FROM
HEROIN
TO
HOPE

MAKING SENSE OF
THE LOSS OF A CHILD

D1508738

From Heroin to Hope
Written by Marsha I. Wiggins, Ph.D.
Copyright © 2018 Marsha I. Wiggins, Ph.D.

ISBN: 978-0-692-11391-2

Published by KoruSpirit, LLC

Cover and book design
Copyright ©2018 John H. Matthews
www.bookconnectors.com

FROM HEROIN TO HOPE

MAKING SENSE OF THE LOSS OF A CHILD

MARSHA I. WIGGINS, Ph.D.

This book is dedicated to my beloved son
Brian Cameron Frame
November 20, 1986-August 9, 2013
May his life be cause for thanksgiving
And may his memory be a blessing.

TABLE OF CONTENTS

PREFACE

TO LOSE A child is heartbreaking. To lose a child as a result of a drug overdose increases the pain exponentially. For parents who experience this type of loss, the silence from others is deafening. The stigma and shame can be debilitating. When I lost my 26-year-old son, Cameron, to heroin, I was devastated. I kept telling myself that as a mental health professional with a Ph.D. and an experienced clergyperson, I *should* have been able to do something to prevent his tragic death. After all, I had tremendous knowledge, training, experience, and faith. And none of it was enough to turn the tide of my son's heroin addiction.

In this book, I provide research-based information about the grief journey and illustrate these concepts by sharing my experience of losing my son, Cameron, to a heroin overdose. This book is written for parents who have lost their children to a drug overdose or other addiction, and for others who have suffered similar losses. It is for mental health professionals who assist grievers in managing the pain of loss. It is for clergy and other spiritual leaders who help mourners make sense of the loss and come to terms with the religious and spiritual aspects of grief. This book is for anyone who wants to understand the tremendous consequences of the heroin epidemic and how it affects families who lose loved ones to an overdose. This book is the story of moving from heroin to hope.

Marsha Wiggins, Ph.D.
May, 2018
West Palm Beach, Florida

Acknowledgements

I would give anything not to have had the horrific experience of losing Cameron—the experience that resulted in the writing of this book. Although this grief has been deeply personal, it has not been private. So many people have also carried the pain that resulted from Cameron's death. And so many have been present for me and offered the love and support that enabled me to speak from my heart about this incredible loss and the ongoing healing journey.

I am grateful to Imara for offering the inspiration and vision for the project. I am indebted to my special friends Sue Giullian and Liz and John Harvey who provided hospitality and a dedicated space for days of uninterrupted writing.

I appreciate the skill and wisdom of those who read, critiqued, and edited the manuscript: Pam Cahoon, Jenn Cook, Liz Harvey, Elizabeth Mallonee, and Ruth Possehl. Special thanks go to my 93-year-old mother, Laura Wiggins, who, despite failing eyesight, edited the entire manuscript. Kudos to Tammie Striggles who provided

Mom with technological assistance. I am grateful to Christopher Hoffmann for proofreading and to John H. Matthews and BookConnectors for the cover design and production.

Thank you to my readers. May these words provide strength, encouragement, and hope for the journey.

CHAPTER 1:
LOSING CAMERON

IN THE EARLY morning hours of August 9, 2013, I received the phone call I had dreaded would come, the phone call somehow I *knew* would come, the phone call no parent ever wants to receive. On the other end of the line was my son's dad, voice trembling, choking back tears, informing me that our precious 26-year-old son, Cameron, was in the ICU on life support as a result of a heroin overdose. After a few seconds of conversation, I realized I was being asked if I would support the doctors' recommendations that they remove the life support. Cameron's brain was so damaged, and his breathing so shallow, it was next to impossible he would ever be able to function apart from the machines and tubes. In the midst of my shock and horror, unable to fully take it all in, I remember hearing my hollow voice speak these words, "Then, we will have to let him go." And every day since I uttered those heartbreaking words, I have been on the journey of letting him go.

I put the phone down and sat in bed, wailing, waiting for

dawn to break, aware that suddenly my life had changed forever. I wondered how my sweet, smart, affectionate, compassionate, fun-loving boy-child had become so lost. Still, I could not grasp the fact that the young man who cared for me so much that once he walked off his job to fix my flat tire could become possessed by the powerful force of heroin—a demon that took his health, his home, his heart, and ultimately his life.

Daybreak brought with it fear, panic, waves of nausea, rage, and shame as I began to make phone calls bearing the devastating news of Cameron's death to family members and friends. The agony and desolation in loved ones' voices as they received the dreadful news led me to this desperate prayer: "Please, please, let me wake up from this horrifying nightmare." These words would become my mantra in the days, weeks, months, and years ahead.

After the phone calls came innumerable arrangements: flights from Florida to Colorado, housing for myself, family, and friends, transportation, meals, appointments with the funeral director, talks with the church pastors and staff, a memorial service. And then there were the gut-wrenching conversations with the people involved first-hand in the tragedy: Cameron's girlfriend in addition to the young woman who found him alone, near death, in a vacant garage. My heart was seared again as I learned my son had been shooting up with a buddy, who, when he realized Cameron had overdosed and was in trouble, fled from the scene. I was enraged that this other young man, also an addict, could not even call 911. Instead, he left my beloved son alone to die. For Cameron, and all those who loved him, death was the last scene in his ongoing drama of being caught in the grip of heroin.

Adopted at birth, Cameron enjoyed many privileges. He was the only child of parents who were fortunate enough to be able to provide him with a stable home, high-quality education, opportunities to learn a variety of sports and skills, summers spent at camp in the Colorado mountains, domestic and international travel, connections with extended family and friends, a supportive church community, boundless love, and a tenacious commitment to parenting him. As a result of these factors, Cameron had less risk for abusing substances than most adolescents. Nevertheless, his father and I learned quickly that despite each of us having a doctoral degree in a mental health field, many years' experience counseling others, and my being an ordained minister, we were no match for the formidable monster called heroin.

Cameron's sense of unworthiness and feeling "less than" must have started in middle school. He struggled academically in elementary school, and his early adolescence was marked by experiences of being bullied, though he was extremely outgoing and had lots of friends. His transition to high school was rocky. He was "getting by" academically, but he never found a niche in his flagship high school of over 3,000 students. He refused to get involved in extracurricular activities. He gained weight. He started smoking at 14. We tried everything. We hired tutors. We considered private school and military school, and finally settled on a smaller, local, public school. We sent him to counseling. We went with him to counseling. We marshaled support from our friends. We insisted he stay involved in the youth group at church. We set boundaries and curfews. We negotiated family contracts. We enforced consequences for breach of contract. Nothing we did seemed to help Cameron gain traction and move forward in his life.

After high school, Cameron's life began spiraling downward. He left college before completing his first semester. He moved back home. He got a series of minimum wage jobs. He moved into an apartment. He began hanging out with people we did not know. He kept his distance, insisting he was "living his own life." He amassed debt. He lost the apartment. He moved back home. He got and lost more jobs. He stayed with first one friend and then another. He looked pale. He lost weight. His eyes were sallow. Their characteristic sparkle was gone.

Finally, I suspected Cameron was using drugs. He admitted to marijuana use. He denied using other drugs. I tried to convince him to stop using. I offered to pay for counseling and substance abuse treatment. He denied he had a problem and tried to assure me he could "handle it." But as time went by, it was obvious to me he was not "handling" it.

By early 2011, I was worried about Cameron's lack of direction, his lack of interest in school, his poor work history, his endless requests that I "lend" him money, his precarious living situation, his inordinate fatigue, his ashen face, his drug use. Contrary to evidence, he claimed he was "OK," "getting by," "figuring it out," and he reminded me he was an adult and didn't want me "meddling" in his business.

In July, 2011, when Cameron was 22, I was making plans to take early retirement from my position as a university professor of counseling and to move home to Florida. As my retirement date grew closer, Cameron grew distant and more aloof. I suspected he felt abandoned by my moving, and I told myself he was staying away to avoid facing the pain of our separation. Somehow, I never suspected he was slipping farther and farther away into the abyss of substance abuse.

Although I had wired Cameron the money for an airline ticket from Colorado to my father's 90th birthday celebration in Florida, my gut told me he would not show up. Despite his promise to be there, I knew he would spend the money on drugs. In January, 2012, as I was leaving for my father's party, Cameron's dad called with devastating news: Cameron had appeared on his doorstep in active heroin withdrawal. He was sick, desperate, and terrified. This news rocked my world. Instead of reveling in the joy of my dad's big day and the celebration with extended family and friends, I steeled myself against the pain, got through the party, and began the frightening and fruitless fight to save my child from destruction and death.

Cameron was admitted to a detox center in Colorado. The next day I began making a series of frantic phone calls to friends and mental health colleagues, searching for help to find the right treatment program and calling in favors to get Cameron admitted to an inpatient program as soon as possible. For the next year and a half, I was consumed by thoughts of Cameron and prayers for his deliverance from his addiction. I was 2000 miles away from him, and I felt helpless knowing my son was moving closer to the brink of disaster with each passing day.

My memories of the months following Cameron's initial detox are a blur of endless phone calls and email updates, moments of hope paired with days of disappointment. A colleague arranged for Cameron to be admitted to a local inpatient program, and I do not think he lasted there 24 hours. He said he felt his privacy was compromised because some of the treatment staff were my former students. The next day, he grabbed his bag and just walked out. When I heard this news, my heart sank. It had taken so much courage for me to make those calls. I had needed to swallow my pride. I had been compelled to acknowledge my son was an addict. Just the thought of that label, "addict," filled me with embarrassment and shame. Who was I to presume to train students in delivering mental health services when I could not prevent my own son's addiction to heroin?

Cameron tried living with his dad. He applied for jobs that didn't involve drug screening. If he applied for a job that did require a drug test, he smuggled in someone else's urine sample. When he did land a job, he never kept it for long. His story about the job loss was that it was always the employer's fault. It always involved Cameron's perception of not being treated fairly. He could never take responsibility for his problems. Each time there was a new report of a job lost, I was overcome by a tsunami of feelings: anger at him for not stepping up and following through; disappointment that we had given him so much and he had wasted his gifts; sadness that his life was in utter chaos; fear he would never get clean and sober; despair that I could not do anything to change the situation. Heroin had taken over his brain, his body. Indeed, it controlled his life.

We learned Cameron was stealing when he got arrested for petty theft. There was a series of burglaries, charges, and jail time. When Cameron was caught stealing, his father insisted he arrange for another place to live. With no money and no job, Cameron spent some nights on friends' couches and in their basements.

On Christmas Eve, 2012, Cameron, now 26, called me on a stranger's cell phone, reporting he was homeless and would be spending a frigid night in a Colorado city park. I hung up from that call and wept. I could not bear to think of my cherished son, my "baby," getting high and passing out on a park bench on Christmas Eve. I felt utterly desolate, horrified that heroin had enslaved my son, despondent at my inability to turn the tide.

I dreaded the phone calls from Colorado with new reports of Cameron's most recent crimes and punishments. I asked myself how I could have raised a delinquent, a felon. As a clergy person, I had made sure Cameron was in church weekly and was surrounded by loving, supportive adults. As a highly educated mental health professional, I was schooled in parenting and substance abuse prevention. As Cameron's life unraveled as a result of his heroin addiction, I felt more and more like an imposter. I told myself that I, of all people, should have caught this problem sooner. I should have insisted on intense therapy and substance abuse treatment way back when he was in middle school. I must have denied, or at best underestimated, the seriousness of Cameron's symptoms because I couldn't accept the notion that *my* son would ever become an addict.

Early in 2013, Cameron's father arranged for him to enter a 90-day residential substance abuse treatment program in another state. I wasn't persuaded such a program would be worth the expense, nor was I that hopeful it would be effective. However, as the days and weeks went by, my conversations with Cameron became more positive. He seemed to be working the program. I began to hear the old lilt in his voice. His humor returned. He kept telling me he loved me. I dared to believe he had turned the corner and would commit himself to staying clean and sober. Cameron completed the rehab program and returned home to Colorado. I flew out to visit him and was thrilled because it seemed as if the *real* Cameron was back. He looked healthy. His eyes were bright. His demeanor was upbeat. He could not stop hugging me.

Not long after I returned to Florida, again my hopes were dashed. Cameron had gotten together with a young woman, also from Colorado, whom he had met in the treatment program. Neither of them was strong enough to resist the siren song of heroin. Together they descended into heroin hell. Again, he entered another residential treatment program. I flew out to Colorado to attend a family therapy session at the facility. After about 10 minutes in the therapy room, Cameron burst into a fit of rage, shouting obscenities. No amount of effort from the therapist or us could calm him. Eventually, before the session was over, Cameron walked out. I was furious with him for leaving the session and not taking his treatment seriously. I felt exhausted and manipulated. And I was losing hope of ever getting my delightful, loving, funny, adventuresome son back.

Cameron's walkout and later refusal to participate in therapy sessions resulted in his being discharged from the treatment program. The insurance company would not pay for Cameron's noncompliance. Cameron was back on the street again doing God-knows-what to stay alive and feed his heroin habit. When I learned of this turn of events, I was livid that the treatment facility staff had not at least referred Cameron to an intensive outpatient program (IOP). I was feeling disheartened about substance abuse treatment in general and terrified for Cameron's safety.

Not long after his dismissal from the treatment program, I discovered Cameron was drug dealing and was involved in more burglary. He stole a computer, a camera, jewelry, and other valuables. Then, he broke into a car and stole someone's wallet. He ended up back in the county jail with more felony charges. There were attorneys and hearings, and postponement of hearings, and one day melted into another. On one hand, I was beside myself with anxiety. "How could *my son* be in jail? What will ever become of him?" On the other hand, I was relieved. I told myself, "He has a roof over his head. He has a warm, dry place to sleep. He is getting three meals a day. He has no access to drugs." Never would I have imagined I would be grateful for Cameron to be in jail.

In the late spring of 2013, I flew back out to Colorado and visited Cameron in jail. My heart disintegrated when I saw him in an inmate's jumpsuit. We had only about 30 minutes. I had to talk to him on a telephone and look at him through a plexiglass window. It felt surreal to see Cameron incarcerated. It felt like we were characters in a crime-focused TV show. I wanted so badly to escape from that bad drama. I longed to hold him, to rescue him, to protect him from the harsh reality of confinement and from the demon of the heroin he still craved. When I was escorted out of the detention center, I had no idea this would be the last time I would see Cameron alive.

In late July of 2013, I was on vacation in the Florida Keys. I was scrolling leisurely through my newsfeed on Facebook and I shrieked when I saw a post from Cameron. I knew it couldn't really be from him. He had no phone. He was in jail. I thought surely someone was playing a cruel joke on me and on all of Cameron's Facebook "friends." When I looked closely at the post, it read, "Holy sh*t! Finally out of jail. Been there since April 18. Wow, this is crazy!!!!" I was the first person to respond to his post. I wrote, "Where are you? Call me!" I never heard from him. A chill of terror ran through my body. "This cannot be good," I remember saying aloud. Suddenly, I felt compelled to find him, to understand what had prompted his release. I needed to know where he was going and where he would sleep that night. It didn't take long to hear the story. Apparently, Cameron had been transferred to another county to address a misdemeanor charge, and when that was complete, the detention center officials had released him. They had simply opened the doors and set him free. He should have been transported back to the previous county to continue serving his time. But that did not happen. Despite countless phone calls to anyone and everyone related to Cameron's case, no one had come forth to prevent his release. In a matter of minutes, gone were the shelter; the warm, dry bed; the meals; the drug-free environment. Again, my beloved, vulnerable son was on the streets hanging out with his old friend, heroin.

When I learned of the latest events, I felt nothing but sheer panic. I was totally distraught, fearful of an overdose, powerless to find or save my lost son. The evening of August 8, 2013, after having made myriad phone calls to Colorado trying desperately to connect with someone who could locate Cameron and assure me he was safe, I said aloud, "I'm going to get a phone call that he's overdosed." The call came that night. Despite all our valiant efforts and the expenditure of thousands of dollars, we had lost our son to drugs—first to marijuana, then to cocaine, then to prescription opioids, and finally to heroin that took his life.

My story of loving and losing Cameron is just a variation on the narratives thousands of parents could write about their children's lost battles with heroin. As the opioid and heroin epidemic grows and spreads, more and more heartbroken parents are initiated into the club they had hoped they would never be forced to join.

She was no longer
Wrestling with the grief,
But could sit down with it
As a lasting companion
And make it a sharer in
Her thoughts.
- George Eliot

With overwhelming grief as my constant companion, I have felt like I was drowning at sea, gasping for breath. I have prayed to be rescued while simultaneously beseeching God to take me, too. In spite of this devastating loss, I have somehow managed to get out of bed every day, to do my work, to engage in meaningful relationships, and to move forward in my life. Perhaps it is because, despite being tossed about in a tempest of grief, I have been given a boat. The boat is built of my amazingly resilient nature, my relentless pursuit of wholeness and joy, my specialized training in theology and counseling, my experience as a pastor and a professor, and by the sheer grace of God. I offer this book as a life buoy for all whose children were lost to heroin and other substances, and to all who feel they are slowly perishing in the turbulent waters of grief. My hope is that in these pages readers will find affirmation and assistance in navigating the treacherous sea of loss. This book is born of unspeakable sorrow. To write it has required me to dive deeply into my own pain to honor my son, Cameron. This book is for all of us treading water in the swift currents of grief. It is for the ones left behind.

Chapter 2:
The Unique Challenges of Losing Our Children to Drugs or Alcohol

The death of any child is a traumatic loss for the child's parents, family members and friends. Our grief is exacerbated by the fact that a child's death contradicts our expectations of when certain life events will occur. Our children are not supposed to predecease us. Psychologists consider the premature death of a child to occur *off time*.[1] This "out of sync" loss challenges our assumptions of how life should unfold, and it threatens our basic sense that life is safe and predictable. As a result, many of us experience more intense, enduring grief than those who lose loved ones *on time*.

We share the disordered timing of our child's death with all other parents who lose their children. However, losing a child to drugs or alcohol is a unique experience because it involves the following dynamics: (a) the stigma surrounding substance abuse, (b) the guilt for not doing more for our child, (c) unconventional grief, (d) the relief at the end of a long fight to save our child and the guilt for feeling relieved, and (e) the sense of having failed as a parent.

The Stigma Surrounding Substance Abuse

Stigma is a mark of disgrace associated with a particular circumstance, quality, or person. When people are labeled by their illness, such as addiction, they are set apart, judged, and stereotyped. Because of stigma, those who use drugs are viewed as "less than," scum of the earth, junkies. But we who are parents see them as our sons and daughters. Such negative attitudes toward people who abuse drugs and alcohol result in prejudice that leads to discrimination. When we are stigmatized because our son or daughter died of drug or alcohol abuse, we may feel shame, blame, hopelessness, distress, and loneliness. In addition, we may stigmatize ourselves because of the cultural beliefs we hold about substance abuse and addiction. We may also experience social exclusion, isolate ourselves from others, and be reluctant to seek help.

During Cameron's battle with heroin, and even after his death by overdose, I found myself feeling ashamed that *my son* suffered and died in this way. It was particularly distressing to disclose these facts to others whose children were exemplars of success. Although everyone who responded to my loss was genuinely sad and sorry I was hurting, I could not help but wonder how different things might have been if Cameron had died from an illness such as cancer. Even though I knew Cameron's addiction was an illness and that his brain had been hijacked by heroin, I considered it a private burden, and I did not seek the help I would have recommended to others.

There are several reasons why there is such a stigma attached to addictions. First, from at least as early as the 19th century, supporters of the moral model of addiction believed drug and alcohol abuse was the result of a character defect. Spurred on by the Prohibition movement in the early 1900s, many people considered addiction to be the result of weakness and lack of willpower. People became addicts because they made poor choices and lacked moral strength. Thus, the response to those wrestling with addictions was to blame them and to suggest they deserved punishment rather than treatment. Sadly, the moral model of addiction persists despite being superseded by the notion of addiction as a disease that involves biological and genetic components.

Second, related to the moral model of addiction is the criminalization of drug activity. When legislatures began imposing criminal sanctions on those who used and sold drugs, the underlying message was drug usage was immoral. Even today, when people with substance use problems commit "crimes" associated with buying, selling, or using drugs, the illegal activity carries with it disgrace and scandal. Moreover, when our children land in jail as a result of criminal acts, more often than not they do not have access to treatment programs, thus delaying their opportunity for recovery. And, because those like Cameron who are addicted to drugs, especially heroin, have persistent cravings, it is not surprising they return immediately to using once they are released from jail. Again, like Cameron, they are more vulnerable to and less tolerant of drugs because of the period of forced abstinence. This post-incarceration drug usage increases the lethality potential and may be one of the reasons why Cameron's death came so quickly after his release from jail.

Third, stigma is also associated with the prevalence of relapse. Although some people with other illnesses such as heart disease or diabetes may change their eating and exercise habits when confronted with potentially negative health outcomes, abstaining from drugs and alcohol is an extremely complex and difficult process. In recent years, researchers, treatment providers, physicians, and drug and alcohol users themselves have learned that recovery involves much more than "just saying no." Ironically, compared to the stigma of drug and alcohol addiction, there is little stigma associated with those who eat pizza or french fries or chocolate cake when they are trying to abstain from these foods to benefit their health. Their relapse is easily dismissed as a normal occurrence. However, heroin addicts who start using again during recovery often are shamed and belittled for their failure to stay clean.

Having never been a substance abuser myself, I have no first-hand experience of the compulsion to use a drug or of the physical need for it. Looking back, I realize I underestimated the difficulty of "kicking" heroin. Even though I had read volumes of material on addiction and had even taken a graduate-level counseling course on the topic, somehow I was unable to empathize adequately with Cameron's enslavement to heroin. I simply could not identify with his tragic inability to escape its hold. Through this horrific grieving process, I have learned that I unwittingly placed stigma on Cameron when I was so fearful for his future and frustrated by his relapses. I blamed him for not being strong enough to resist heroin's power. I underestimated how hard rehab could be. I began to think of him as a junkie and "ne'er-do-well." I fell into the stigma trap myself. Not only can we unknowingly stigmatize our sons and daughters, but we also internalize the stigma so we believe we are pathetic parents if we raised a son or daughter who has an addiction.

Fourth, stigma toward substance use and abuse is part of the fabric of North American culture. Some of it grows out of both the moral view of addictions and the Prohibition movement. Some of it emerges from preconceived notions about who abuses substances. Our prejudices about race, gender, ethnicity and social class may be another reason stigma exists. Too often we consider substance users and abusers to be men of color, usually African American or Latino, from poor neighborhoods. It is no surprise, then, that White middle-class people who use and abuse substances are stigmatized. Stigma is deeply imbedded in both racism and classism.

One of the aspects of our healing may involve efforts to reduce stigma surrounding drug use. Researchers believe stigma reduction occurs through protest, education, and contact.[2] When we *protest* stigma, we acknowledge it as an unjust and disrespectful attitude toward people who are struggling with a disease. Our efforts to reduce stigma in this way honor our children. *Education* is a vehicle through which we challenge inaccurate stereotypes and misinformation. We replace these judgment errors with accurate facts grounded both in current research and in our own valid experiences. *Contact* involves face-to-face interactions with people in society at large, sharing our stories about our children and their battles with substances. As the public is exposed to the truth of our experiences, we participate in reducing stigma and opening the way to empathy.

Feeling Guilty for Not Doing Enough

Almost all people who have lost a son or daughter to an overdose wish they had done more to save their child. Even when parents have emptied their retirement funds, sold valuables, and taken second mortgages on their homes to pay for treatment, they still end up feeling like they failed their child. Further, some parents spend inordinate amounts of time searching for and evaluating treatment options, getting up in the middle of the night to pick up their son or daughter from an isolated street corner, paying for their child's apartment, food, clothing, or medical bills, bailing him or her out of jail, hiring attorneys, and running interference with law enforcement and the courts. Other parents set firm boundaries with their children who are using drugs. They forbid them to live at home, they cut off financial support, they refuse to bail them out, and embark on an agenda of "tough love" in hopes the consequences of their clear boundaries will motivate their children to stop using. Many parents vacillate between hovering and distancing. They are panic-stricken when they consider what could happen if they don't use all their resources toward their child's recovery, and while doing so, they worry themselves sick over the possibility that they may be enabling and reinforcing the drug-using behavior.

During the early years of Cameron's drug use, I made some attempts at intervention. I arranged for him to see counselors. I "lent" him money. I paid him to do odd jobs around the house. I encouraged him to go to school. I typed his papers. I contacted friends and colleagues to help him get jobs. I paid for him to see a career counselor. Mostly, though, I minimized the seriousness of his substance use, attributing it to adolescent experimentation. Later, in the last months of his life, I was living in Florida and he was in Colorado. Much of that time he was in a treatment program out of state or in jail. During the periods when I knew he was using heroin, I felt powerless to stop it. I sent care packages to him at the detention center. I wrote letters encouraging him to take stock of his life and make a commitment to recovery. I pleaded with colleagues who themselves had been in recovery for years to mentor him. I traveled to visit him and to attend therapy sessions with him. I prayed fervently for a miracle or for divine intervention. None of it was enough. I felt completely incapable of helping him exorcise the demon of heroin. Like other parents of substances users, I felt guilty.

Regardless of what we have done or not done in an effort to rescue our children from the clutch of drugs or alcohol, most of us feel guilty that we did not do enough. We tell ourselves it was our responsibility as parents to take care of our children and to protect them from danger. Even when they are adults, as Cameron was when he died, we never cease believing we must keep them safe. This pervasive sense of failing our children can result in self-blame; it can deepen our grief and hinder our healing.

Grieving Someone Alive

When our children were using drugs or alcohol, we may have experienced unconventional grief. This form of grief is the result of our children becoming people we no longer know or recognize. Unconventional grief can be known as "grieving someone alive." Grieving someone alive is a bit different from the anticipatory grief that occurs when a loved one has a terminal illness or is elderly and we know death is certainly coming. Parents of children who use substances, especially heroin, may experience unconventional grief when they must face the reality that their child is still present as the person they once knew, but psychologically the child is a different person from before. What is particularly painful is that parents have no control over their child's suffering.

When we experience unconventional grief, it can be because our children had a dramatic shift in personality. Their behavior may have become erratic, they may have become involved in criminal activity, their hygiene may have suffered, and their appearance and health may have deteriorated. Many parents grieve for the life their children were not living because they were living for their addiction. The potential lethality of heroin and the epidemic of deaths from its use may have caused our unconventional grief because we worried it was just a matter of time before our child was lost to a heroin overdose. Unconventional grief carries with it some of the same feelings as conventional grief but does so with a different twist. Unconventional grief creates a variety of different feelings. We may have experienced anger at our child's addiction. We may also have felt helplessness because we couldn't do anything to stop it. We may have been fearful of our child's potential death. We may have been shaken by anxiety about when and how the death might come. Certainly we experienced sadness when we contemplated the real possibility of the death of our child who was using substances. There was no end to our disappointment about the possible loss of our child's future and our dreams of what that future could be.

To love an addict is to run out of tears.
- Sandy Swenson
sandyswenson.com

When Cameron was not in rehab or in jail, I was overcome by unconventional grief. I was preoccupied with his safety and filled with fear that he would die of an overdose. While I wanted to remain hopeful that he would commit to recovery and be successful, I experienced many sleepless nights ruminating about losing him. Even when I was with him, I felt extreme sadness because of the person he had become. The mischievous smile had vanished, the compassionate helping had disappeared, and warmth and affection were missing. In their place were surly sneers, obscene language, an unkempt appearance, distance and suspicious hypervigilance. He *looked* a lot like the same person, but he was not at all like the son I knew. Of course I never stopped loving him or praying for his recovery. It was just that I could not believe my delightful son had been transformed into a monster.

Feeling Relief After the Loss and Guilt for Feeling Relieved

When we lose our children to a drug overdose, we are heartbroken. Often their death marks the end of a long, painful, exhausting war in which drugs are the victors. When we have finally emptied our arsenal and laid down our weapons, we are struck by the grim fact that there is no need to fight this particular battle any longer. Gone are the recovery programs, gone are the horrendous nights of wondering where our child could be. Gone is the endless drain on our resources. Gone are the phone calls to attorneys and probation officers. Gone are the visits to the jail. Gone are the sleepless nights when our thoughts are spinning out of control with worry. Gone is the duty to balance the needs of our child on drugs with the needs of our other children. When we lose a child to drugs or alcohol, we set down one of our enormous burdens. In the aftermath of our child's death, we feel a strange relief. We can stop holding our breath and exhale. We know the pain that accompanied the drug use is over. We trust our son or daughter finally is at peace. However, in the instant we release all that has weighed us down and kept us preoccupied for months or years or decades, we pick up another burden: guilt over feeling relieved.

This relief seems wrong, like a betrayal, and we dare not speak too freely about it, lest we be judged as unfeeling or cruel. What we may not know or have forgotten is we are capable of experiencing more than one emotion simultaneously. These feelings are not mutually exclusive. We can feel both relief that the suffering has ended and devastating sadness at the loss of the child we loved so deeply.

After Cameron's death, I felt a huge sense of relief from the constant worry, hypervigilance, and distress his heroin use had created for me. And I felt inconsolable in losing him. It did not take long to begin to feel a twinge of guilt about feeling relieved. Even though I did not have to navigate so many of the day-to-day demands and drama, my distance from the situation and the not knowing created immense anxiety for me. Fortunately, I knew from my counselor training and my work as a therapist and a pastor that mixed emotions were a normal response to such a loss, so I was able to be gentle with myself as I responded to the tragedy. By "being gentle," I mean I was able to give myself permission to be sad, to be tired, to make mistakes. I forgave myself for not having the stamina I used to possess or to be as productive as I had been prior to Cameron's death. I allowed myself to move more slowly. I refused to feel guilty for not wanting to socialize as much in the immediate aftermath of Cameron's death. I took comfort in silence and nature and music. Even though I was able to do these things for myself, it was hard. I required constant reminding that it was okay to take it easy and allow grief to have its way with me.

Believing We Have Failed as Parents and Our Children are "Bad Kids"

When we lose a child to drugs or alcohol, it is easy to assume their substance use is our fault. We tell ourselves (and we may hear from others) if we were "good" parents, our child would not have succumbed to the lure of substances. Or we use the corollary, if they were "good" kids, they would have avoided the trap of addiction. This type of thinking is grounded in the assumption that substance use is the result of a flaw in the parents or the children or both. When we blame ourselves for our child's addiction, we are subscribing (at least in part) to the moral model of addiction described above. This self-blame further solidifies the stigma, shame and guilt we experience.

Even when we acknowledge that none of us is a perfect parent, we may still tell ourselves our child could have been substance free if we had just done a better job of parenting. This assumption is a fallacy. We all know children who had what one might characterize as abusive or neglectful parents who, perhaps, were substance users themselves. Many of these children grew up to be responsible adults without addictions. And we know parents who read every book on parenting, went to parenting classes, used age-appropriate discipline, supported each other, set boundaries, and consistently enforced consequences. Yet, their children experimented with substances and formed habits that were impossible to break.

I am an imperfect mom. Imperfect parenting
does not cause addiction. If that were so, every
child would grow up to be an addict.
- Sandy Swenson
sandyswenson.com

Certainly there exists a genetic predisposition to addiction. It is easy to see the patterns of substance use across the generations. But one never knows if that pattern will be triggered in one's offspring. Unless parents shared drugs and alcohol with their children and encouraged their experimentation with substances, it is a gross generalization to suggest that they are to blame for the addiction. Some people try a drug out of curiosity, and it ends there. Others become addicted after their first introduction to a substance. It all depends on how their brains are wired, what types of trauma they may have undergone, and how they respond to the substance.

In addition, there are personality traits, environmental factors such as type of community and peer influence, level of risk-taking behavior, the presence of other mental health problems, sensitivity to stress, and the drug-induced effects. All of these factors, in concert with an individual's decision-making processes, contribute to substance abuse and addiction. To blame ourselves or to denigrate our parenting is to take far more responsibility and control than legitimately belongs to us. We did not necessarily *fail* as parents, and our children were not inherently "bad." A complex web of circumstances, including genetic vulnerability and our son or daughter's choices, created the addiction that cost them their lives.

Cameron was adopted, so I am unsure of his family history, though the social worker reported it included alcoholism. Though we made many mistakes and fell far from perfection in our parenting, both Cameron's father and I had strong backgrounds in child development and parenting methods. We practiced intentional, psychologically-sound parenting strategies. And we loved our son prodigiously. But we could not control his substance use, and we could not save his life. Despite all I know and believe about the components of Cameron's addiction and subsequent death, from time to time I catch myself asking, "Where did I go wrong?" Part of my healing journey is not to wallow in self-blame, but to acknowledge the many factors that led to this tragic loss.

Those of us who have lost a child to drugs or alcohol share many of the same experiences as other parents whose children have died. Nevertheless, the unique confluence of stigma, guilt, relief and the guilt for feeling relieved, and self-blame can make our grief process more complicated and our suffering more severe.

Questions for Reflection:

» How have you experienced stigma related to your child's substance abuse?

» How have you responded to the stigma?

» What has it been like for you to feel like you did not do enough for your child?

» In what ways have you felt you were grieving someone alive?

» To what degree have you experienced relief that the battle with drugs or alcohol is over?

» What is it like for you to feel guilty for feeling relieved?

» How can you tell a different story about your loss besides that of failing at parenting and raising a "bad" kid?

CHAPTER 3:
THE GRIEF JOURNEY

MOST PEOPLE WHO have been exposed to information on grief and loss are familiar with Kubler-Ross's five stages of grief: *denial, anger, bargaining, depression, and acceptance.*[1] In the first stage, *denial*, we tell ourselves that this terrible loss cannot be happening. This temporary denial protects us from the shock of loss and helps us pace ourselves for coming face to face with death. In the second stage, *anger*, our pain gains momentum and bursts forth as anger toward friends, family, and the deceased. We are outraged that our loved one has died, and we feel betrayed by the death. In the third stage, *bargaining*, we try to regain control by asking "what if" and asserting "if only." We may ask, "What if he had stayed in rehab longer? What if he hadn't gone out that night with drug-using friends?" Or we may lament, "If only the Narcan had been available. If only someone had found him sooner." These mind games are efforts to stave off the pain and often end up making us feel guilty for not having saved our child. In the fourth stage, *depression*, we feel deep sadness because of our loss and come to realize we have to say goodbye. In the fifth and final stage, *acceptance*, we come to terms with our loss and begin the challenge of living with that loss.

For decades this linear model explaining a universal process of how people coped with loss was the accepted wisdom on the topic. What some people are not aware of is that Kubler-Ross intended these stages to describe what people who knew they were *dying* experienced. Over time, the stages were applied to grievers as well.

In the previous chapter, I discussed unconventional grief and described what it is like to be the parent of a child addicted to drugs or alcohol. I explained how difficult it was to vacillate between hope for Cameron's recovery and fear of his death from an overdose. In some ways, I experienced Kubler-Ross's stages of grief: *denial* Cameron had a problem as serious as it was; *anger* at him and his group of peers for wasting their gifts, their resources, their lives on drugs; *bargaining* with Cameron and myself and perhaps even God, offering to do *anything* to get him to stop using drugs; *depression* because of how helpless and hopeless I felt as Cameron sank deeper into his addiction and no amount of rehab seemed to help him turn his life around; and a touch of *acceptance* that I could potentially lose Cameron to a drug overdose.

As researchers and mental health providers studied the phenomenon of grief, they discovered it was much more complex than Kubler-Ross's stage model. They began to attend to mourners' experiences in their various contexts and relationships. They uncovered many facets of how people learn to live with loss. They learned there was no magic process of grief recovery. They found no "one-size-fits-all" timetable for reconciling the loss. They became aware that other deaths and losses that occurred in close proximity to a major loss could trigger further intense grief reactions. They realized most people who suffered significant losses, even those who lost their children to drugs or alcohol, accommodated to these losses, moved forward in their lives, and still retained a bond with the ones they had lost.

As a result of these investigations into how people dealt with death and other losses, new models of the grief process emerged. These newer models share common themes including: (a) doubt about a universal, predictable path from emotional instability to recovery, (b) movement away from the notion that healthy mourners gave up their connection with the deceased, (c) added focus on the importance of *thoughts* as well as feelings in the grief process, (d) increased sensitivity to unique grief practices informed by specific communities and cultures, (e) a stronger focus on the need for mourners to refashion their sense of who they are in light of the losses, (f) an acknowledgement of the potential for mourners' growth after surviving particularly difficult or traumatic losses, and (g) a broader perspective on how losses are managed in families and other social arenas.[2]

The 6 R Process Model

One of the newer grief models, the 6 R Process Model, developed primarily by Therese Rando,[3] focuses on both grief phases and tasks that most people experience. Although her model did not focus specifically on the death of a child, it is nevertheless applicable. Rando noted as people navigate their grief journey, some return to various phases and tasks and address them again. She did not claim the model is predictive of how everyone will experience grief. In fact, one of the sure truths about grief is that it is unpredictable. However, in this model she described some of the common threads mourners experience as they cope with grief. Rando said the tasks associated with grieving include recognizing and accepting the loss, reacting to the pain of separation, reminiscing about the deceased, relinquishing old attachments, readjusting to the new reality of life without our loved one, and reinvesting in other relationships and new dimensions of life.[4]

When we recognize and accept our loss, we come to terms with the grim reality that our child is gone and will never return. In this phase, it is common to experience denial and to expect to wake up from this horrible nightmare. At this point, denial is not such a bad thing. Actually, it is self-protective. It is a means of survival. It allows us to take in what has happened and, in our own time, begin to respond to it. Accompanying this phase are feelings of being overwhelmed, unmoored from reality, and panic-stricken because our world has been so shaken that we hardly know who we are or what we can expect. For some, anxiety seems to rule, and we become hypersensitive to our environment. Anything can make us nervous, including excessive noise, crowding, or unexpected changes in surroundings. In addition to these occurrences, some people become preoccupied with their deceased child and cannot focus on anything else. Sometimes the preoccupation is based on a fear of not remembering the child's face or voice or worrying the child will become lost to us forever, even in memory. Although some preoccupation with one's deceased child is expected, a prolonged obsession that interferes with attending to activities of daily living, taking care of other children, or going to work can be a sign of the need for more support or professional help.

After that chilling midnight phone call when I first learned of Cameron's death, I could not fully comprehend the fact that my beloved son was dead. I suspect that being 2000 miles away from him and not faced with the ghastly reality of the hospital and doctors and the removal of life support made it easier for me to be caught up in denial. I felt as if I were living in a fog, floating through the first few horrific days that required travel, arrangements, meetings, and so many decisions. My entire body alternated between feeling totally numb and excruciating pain. My memory was unreliable, and as a result I felt unsteady and afraid I would never regain my sense of self. Moreover, any source of what I considered excessive noise (e.g. music, TV, people talking loudly in restaurants) was intolerable to me. I could not bear to be exposed to a noisy environment. Nor could I bear being in a crowded room. In those first days and weeks, I felt like I just might suffocate. In fact, I had to remind myself to breathe.

When we allow ourselves to react to the loss and experience the pain, we face the fact that we can no longer steel ourselves against the chaos the death of our child has created. The confrontation with the reality of our loss evokes a variety of intense emotions: anger, rage, guilt, and sorrow. We may experience times when we feel emotionally out of control, worried we will not be able to manage our anger or outbursts. We may be paralyzed by all kinds of guilt: guilt over anything we can dream up that we believe may have led to our child's addiction; guilt over not recognizing the problem sooner; guilt over failed interventions to stop the drug abuse; guilt over not being able to prevent this untimely and tragic death. Other times, we find ourselves sobbing, wondering if we will ever be able to stop the tears. It is completely normal to want to avoid our pain and to escape from such excruciating agony that keeps us feeling emotionally raw and wounded. However, slowly we discover that allowing ourselves to experience and express our deepest feelings creates a release in tension that is ultimately healing.

When we investigate, we find beneath the grief of anger a reservoir of sadness, and beneath the sadness, an ocean of love beyond our wildest dreams.
– Stephen Levine, *Unattended Sorrow*[4]

As the painful reality of Cameron's death began to pierce my protective emotional armor, I felt enraged, and found myself prostrate, pounding the floor with my fists in anger at his tragic, senseless, and preventable death. When I wasn't thrashing about on the floor, I was shaking my fists at the sky—all signs of how out of control I felt, and how angry and bereft I felt all at the same time. And then there were the tears. Sometimes they seemed to leak from the corners of my eyes without warning. Other times, I would sob wildly, frightening myself with the fear of never being able to regain composure. These emotional expressions have been exhausting on one hand and cleansing on the other. They have been doorways through which I have been able to release emotions that make me feel tense and immobilized. They have taught me about the power of surrender and the blessing of entering into the pain of loss.

> *"I shall look at the world through tears. Perhaps I*
> *shall see things that dry-eyed I could not see."*[6]
> – Nicolas Wolterstorff, *Lament for a Son*

When we remember our children, share stories of their lives, gather with those who knew and loved them, and keep their memory alive, we are practicing reminiscing. Looking at photos or other mementos and displaying items with special meaning provide opportunities for us to gather up the whole of our children's lives—not just the achingly difficult tales of their addictions. Some people find writing about their memories of their child can be comforting. Keeping a journal of grief experience can document our sojourn through the process.

After Cameron's death, I pored over the huge stack of photo albums I had carefully and lovingly created over the years, painstakingly labeling and dating each one. I was forced to smile through my tears as I opened the first album to the photo of a 10-foot-tall wooden stork friends had placed in our yard when we welcomed Cameron into our lives as an infant. I giggled at the shot of Cameron at two, sitting on a potty chair engrossed in the newspaper comics. I beamed with pride at 8-year-old Cameron perched on the top of a large rock pinnacle in Rocky Mountain National Park after a hike. I delighted in the photos from our trips all over the United States and to various locations throughout Europe, as Cameron's 11-year-old cheerful countenance stared back at me from so many beautiful spots. I reveled in the accomplishment that shone on Cameron's face at significant moments such as his church confirmation, his high school graduation, his completion of the first 90-day drug rehab program. And I anguished as I observed the more recent photos that revealed my young-adult son who was so terribly lost and sinking into the despair of his heroin addiction. As I looked at hundreds of pictures of my son, I was overcome by waves of nostalgia and grief. And I realized how Cameron's life was so much more than his addiction. I resolved to remember *all* of his story—not just the tragic series of events that culminated in his untimely death.

At first, this idea of relinquishing or letting go of our child seems impossible and undesirable. We cannot imagine how such an act could be in our best interest. However, we come to understand that we do not ever lose the love we feel for our children or the place they hold in our hearts. Instead, we loosen the ties we had when our children were living, and we begin to move forward, learning to live without them. We find ourselves awakened to a new world where we cannot assume we will have visits with our child, share holidays and meals, and enjoy the intertwining of their life with ours. This phase requires us to accept our children's new and unwelcomed status as deceased, to give up some of the assumptions about how our life's trajectory would unfold, and to make a commitment to move forward in our lives without their physical presence.

Letting go of Cameron's earthly presence in my life has been especially challenging because for 26 years my role as his mother was an integral part of my identity. Having to redefine myself and to forge a future without him is something I never dreamed I would have to do. Losing my only child has shaken the entire foundation of my world. As so many parents who have lost children have asked, I, too, asked myself, "Am I a parent if I no longer have a child?" I have had to wrestle with the crushing truth of not having anyone to whom I can leave family keepsakes. I have had to accept the disappointment of never having grandchildren. And even though many children never end up being caregivers for their aging parents, I am well aware that with Cameron's death, he will never be my caregiver. Relinquishing has brought with it the dismay of discarding boxes of my own treasures. It has forced me to reckon with meaning I craft in the present and the future rather than relying on what was stockpiled in the past. Though I carry Cameron with me in my heart, his life and his needs no longer impinge on mine in the present. Part of *relinquishing* has included relinquishing the torture I endured because of Cameron's addiction. It has meant releasing the fear and the anxiety. It has enabled me to experience some measure of peace because he is at peace.

To reinvest is to make a place in our lives for the incredible loss of our children, to adapt to the profound change this loss has brought to us, and to take a chance on life again. We don't ever "get over" or graduate from our grief. We know all too well time *does not* heal all wounds. We carry these wounds with us alongside our new life. We move forward into an unknown future, accommodating the loss and accepting the specific changes it has required of us. In order to be transformed by grief, we make an effort to make meaning out of our most devastating losses. In this way, we may acknowledge a newfound strength, we may invest in new relationships and enterprises, and we may understand more acutely the fragility of life.

Cameron's death has called me into a new way of being in the world. It has deepened my empathy for those who walk on similar paths of sorrow. It has opened me to exploring ways I can use my loss experience to guide others. As I age, I am being forced to consider a future without my son. Such a reality makes me more reliant on networks of support, "chosen family," and the risk-taking involved in new relationships and adventures. It is a reality I would never have chosen, and yet it invites me to know myself and to understand others more deeply. In essence, this phase of grief has required not only readjusting and reinvesting, it has provided the opportunity to reinvent myself. The crises of Cameron's heroin addiction and subsequent death have contained both pain and possibility. I have experienced both.

From Loss to Restoration and Back Again

In the Dual Process Model, Margaret Stroebe and Henk Schut[7] described how people cope with the death of a loved one. Their assumption is that when people are able to use certain strategies to tolerate the pain of loss, they are better able to adapt to that loss. Stroebe and Schut challenged the popular notion that people have to do "grief work," that is, confronting the loss of death and entering into an intense period of bereavement in order to come to terms with loss and to live healthy lives on the other side of it. They claimed bereavement involves going back and forth between loss-orientation and restoration-orientation. In the case of the death of a child, loss-orientation is about the ache in our hearts when we lose a child, and it involves the story of what happened and how vacant we feel without our son or daughter. Restoration-orientation is about what we have to do to survive in the new world we now inhabit. Restoration-orientation may involve tasks associated with our child's belongings, dealings with our child's spouses or significant others, and possibly our grandchildren, or it may involve attending to legal or financial concerns.

Stroebe and Schut honored the uniqueness of each person's experience and assured us that our vacillation is perfectly normal. Thus, healthy grieving involves both negative and positive feelings and activities as well as confrontation and avoidance of grieving. Gradually, over time, more focus is on the restoration-orientation and less on the loss-orientation. It is the oscillation between loss and restoration that enables one to adapt to the tragic death of a child.

After the news of Cameron's death, I was reeling emotionally. I fluctuated from disbelief, to rage, to guilt, to anguish. But I could not stay for too long in the misery that accompanied my distress. I had to take care of things in my "regular" life, such as work responsibilities, household tasks, and family needs. I found myself needing to put the emotional heartbreak on a shelf now and then just to attend to the activities of living in my shattered world. At first, I became self-critical, thinking I was not honoring my son if I were taking a break from the tears and balancing my checkbook, or if I were attending to details of a professional meeting. Somehow I believed I was not grieving properly if I were not curled up in a fetal position in bed with the covers pulled tightly over my head. Granted, there were moments when I wanted nothing more than to drown in despondency, but much of the time I would alternate between intense pain and an emotional "mini-vacation" that allowed me to accomplish the mundane requirements of everyday life. This vacillation between loss and restoration is the heart of the dual process model. Now I understand that my experience of confrontation and avoidance was more healing than harmful. In fact, researchers who studied Stroebe and Schut's dual process model among parents dealing with the death of a child found a loss-orientation focus predicted poorer psychological adjustment than restoration-orientation. They found that high levels of restoration-orientation offset the depression associated with loss-orientation.[8]

Not Grieving Is Not An Option

One of the most important things we learn from all of the phases, models, and tasks of grieving is that they all carry some truth, and there is no one right way to grieve. What is clear, however, is that in order to move forward in our lives and adapt to the gut-wrenching loss of our child, we must allow ourselves to feel the pain, take breaks from it, focus on rebuilding our lives, and to keep walking the path, however circuitous it may be.

When one attempts stoically to avoid grief or stuffs it away inside, it is a far more dangerous choice than letting it out. When we try to keep our sorrow at bay, it finds a way to demand attention. It is much like trying to affix a screen protector to a mobile device. We press down on the first air pocket, smoothing it out, thinking we have eliminated the air bubble, only to discover it pops up somewhere else. Such is the nature of grief we try to push away—it, too, surfaces somewhere else in our bodies, our minds, our behaviors, or our relationships.

Keeping ourselves busy constantly so we don't have time to dwell on our loss can take a toll on us too. We crowd our minds with facts and figures and lists and plans so there is no room for thoughts of the tragic death of our child. At the end of the day, we fall into bed exhausted and spent, and then our grief haunts our dreams and disturbs our sleep.

One of the pitfalls of grief avoidance is the ferocious desire to numb oneself from the unrelenting pain. Turning to alcohol or drugs to dull the persistent ache in our chest is, ironically, exactly what took our children from us. The paradox is we both hate the drugs and can now understand in part the lure of their hollow promise to offer us deliverance from suffering. The fact is that there is no deliverance from suffering when we lose our children. For the ones left behind, it is not possible to go over, under or around the pain. The only path is to go through it.

As we walk the path of grief, we discover that each of us has our own process, and no two people (not even the parents of the same deceased child) grieve alike. Over time, we discern that there is no timeline for grief. It is not a terrible experience that is eventually "over" like an invasive medical test or a night spent sleeping on the floor in an airport. No, we are forever changed and refashioned by the death of our children. And, despite whatever misguided "wisdom" we may receive from well-meaning friends or family, we will never "get over it." Instead, we will always carry the loss with us, even though we may not think about it or speak about it every day. It will continue to shape our lives in the present and the future.

QUESTIONS FOR REFLECTION

» In what ways have you experienced the denial, anger, bargaining, depression and acceptance associated with Kubler-Ross's stages of grief?

» How have you experienced the 6 Rs: recognizing the loss, reacting to separation, reminiscing about the deceased, relinquishing old attachments, readjusting and reinvesting? What have these phases been like for you?

» How have you moved back and forth between an orientation toward loss and one toward restoration? What feelings have been associated with each of these orientations?

» How have you been tempted to avoid grieving? What have you done to give yourself permission to experience deeply this profound loss?

Chapter 4:
The Physical, Emotional, Social, Mental, and Spiritual Toll of Grieving

GRIEVING IS EXHAUSTING. It wrings from us the physical stamina and the emotional strength we usually have and makes us much more physically and emotionally fragile than we may have been prior to our child's death. We can be surprised by both the intensity with which we experience certain emotions and by the numbness that dulls us to feelings that sometimes are overwhelming. Grief makes us more physically and emotionally vulnerable than we might be under "normal" circumstances.

Moreover, grief can be socially isolating. People who are not grieving with us may feel uncomfortable being around us and may withdraw because they feel awkward talking about our deceased child. They may be experiencing some irrational fear that associating with us makes them more likely to lose their children. In addition, when we are in the pit of grief, we aren't likely to want to socialize in ways we did before our child died. Again, everyone is different on this point, but it is very common for us to pull away from social contacts and to believe others don't want to be burdened by our sorrow.

As if feeling emotionally depleted, physically tired, and socially reclusive were not enough, we may also feel mentally sluggish. The fog that settles in our brains after the heart-rending death of our child makes us wonder if we are going crazy or losing our minds. We find it hard to concentrate, difficult to remember things, frustrating not to be able to pay attention, challenging to finish tasks, and daunting to undertake projects that used to be second nature.

A significant loss, like the death of our child, and the subsequent grief that circumscribes our lives, may take a heavy toll on our spiritual well-being also. Because the unthinkable has happened, we are not sure we can trust any of our old assumptions about human life and what gives it meaning. Regardless of our religious or spiritual background and practices (or the lack of them), the heart-rending death of our child usually leaves us with more questions than answers. Well-meaning friends and family may attempt to comfort us with platitudes such as, "He's in a better place now," "God called her home," or "It was God's will." We may find some measure of comfort given the good intentions behind these phrases, but many of us bristle or even become enraged in response to comments that feel like Band-Aids on our broken hearts. The truth is, more often than not, we will be forced to examine and reexamine all we have held true about life, death, God or a higher power, and the afterlife. And we must begin to reflect on these questions while we are physically and emotionally drained, cognitively challenged, and socially isolated.

After Cameron's death, I was appalled at how physically exhausted I was almost every day, all day long. Over my entire adult life, I have had incredible stamina. I have been able to engage in intense workouts, to juggle many work projects simultaneously, to manage the demands of a home, parenting, extended family obligations, and a large social network of friends and acquaintances. In the space of less than 24 hours after I got the news about Cameron, I felt as if my life energy and physical hardiness had been sucked out of me. It was a strain to get out of bed, to get in the shower, to decide what clothes to wear and what to eat. Going to the gym was impossible. I wondered how I would muster the vitality to overcome the downward pull of lethargy to accomplish the minimum requirements and activities of daily living.

Emotionally, I felt spent too. The initial shock of Cameron's death, punctuated by periods of sobbing and rage, was exhausting and unfamiliar. Being someone who has always prided herself on being emotionally grounded, I felt that I was spinning out of control. The range of feelings was totally unpredictable. I was on a roller coaster ride with seemingly no end. All my senses appeared to be either heightened or dulled. Bright light was an assault on my eyes. Noisy environments were intolerable.

Food tasted like Styrofoam. Sometimes my skin ached from being touched. Moreover, the mild anxiety I had previously experienced in crowds grew exponentially. I could not bear to be surrounded by a throng of people. I felt trapped and claustrophobic. Fortunately, most of these sensitivities have waned over time, and my emotions have become less mercurial and erratic.

Even though I am extremely extroverted and usually draw energy from social interaction, after Cameron's death I found myself sapped from being with people. I did not want to be around those whose superficial chatter annoyed me or whose lack of empathy was excruciating. I did, however, feel drawn to those closest to me, and I seemed to absorb their positive energy as I found myself surrounded by love and acceptance. Special friends buoyed me when they sat with me in silence, knowing no words were needed. These relationships kept me afloat during the times I felt like I was drowning in grief.

In the immediate aftermath of Cameron's death, I found that my mind was surrounded by a mental murkiness that was extremely troubling. Having relied on my mental acuity and strong cognitive ability to manage most of life's previous challenges, I felt utterly betrayed when I stumbled with logical processes and rational responses. My memory, also a sharp tool in my arsenal of resources, failed me on numerous occasions, forgetting work-related facts or neglecting to pay bills. Fortuitously, my counseling training had made me aware of the mental haze often associated with grief; therefore, it wasn't as terrifying to me as it could have been otherwise. And, over time, the fog lifted and my mental keenness returned to a large degree; nevertheless, lapses still occur.

In the wake of Cameron's death, my spirituality has been one of my strongest assets. Having been blessed with the opportunity to earn a degree in theology and to work with people who are grieving in my roles as both a clergyperson and a counselor, I had knowledge and experience on my side. In my early adulthood, I had been forced to wrestle with some difficult religious and spiritual questions through my studies and my work. As a result, I did not undergo a crisis of faith when Cameron died of a heroin overdose. On the contrary, my spiritual experience and beliefs enabled me to trust that even in the "valley of the shadow of death" all would yet be well.

I realize that not everyone has the benefit of the background and experience I had. Some people struggle mightily with questions of faith, and they feel extraordinarily lost in a spiritual abyss that brings no comfort. These feelings are common and normal. Staying present in the grief experience and living with the discomfort is part of navigating the grief journey.

Practicing Self-Care in the Grief Process

Given grief's debilitating attacks on our physical, emotional, social, mental, and spiritual well-being, the only antidote to the barrage of ailments is to practice intentional self-care in all of these areas. Living with loss demands that we plan a counter-insurgence that aims to build long-term, holistic support and resources. Given our vulnerability on all sides, we simply cannot leave our overall health and well-being to chance.

Physical Self-Care

The physical demands of responding to the death of our child are exhausting. We lose our appetites or we overeat. We lose sleep or we can't get out of bed. Our immune systems are pushed to their limits when we are grieving. Therefore, to protect our health for the long term, taking care of our physical needs is essential. As much as we may struggle with food intake, being vigilant about what we eat is critical. When we are in the throes of grief, it is not particularly the best time to take on a new diet; however, being judicious about eating healthful food is important. While we may be drawn to comfort foods like ice cream, fast foods, and soda and allow ourselves a treat from time to time, choosing to eat lean meats, fruits, and vegetables will ensure we have the physical strength to fight illness and get through the demands of the difficult days.

Exercise, too, helps protect our health and refuel our energy that is so easily depleted when we are grieving. Even though some days we feel we can hardly put one foot in front of the other, even mild to moderate exercise can make us more alert and elevate our mood. More intense exercise, if we are fit enough, can be a means whereby we release tension and pent-up emotions.

Getting the right amount of sleep during the grief process is at once crucial and challenging. It is not uncommon for our sleep to be disturbed by intrusive thoughts, dreams, and images, especially if our child's death was particularly traumatic. We can experience a flood of thoughts that run like a ticker tape through our minds and rob us of precious hours of sleep. Or, we can fall into bed exhausted, sleep soundly for a few hours, only to find ourselves wide awake at 4:00 a.m. certain we will not sleep another wink that night. Or, we can feel so sad and depressed that we can do nothing but sleep and we struggle with getting out of bed and tackling the tasks of daily life. Whatever sleep disturbances we experience, doing everything in our power to establish a healthy sleep routine will contribute to our well-being in all areas of our life.

Sleep experts suggest establishing specific daily practices to improve one's ability to sleep. They advise us to go to bed and get up at the same time every day, including weekends. They also suggest we turn off our electronic devices at least an hour before bedtime because the light they emit interferes with our ability to shut down our bodies and prepare for sleep. Good sleep hygiene involves not watching intense or violent TV programs or movies or tackling emotionally or mentally demanding work tasks before bed because they may cause us to be more keyed up at a time when we ought to be calming our minds. It is important not to exercise too intensely in the evening because exercise, too, invigorates the body rather than relaxes it. Reducing caffeine intake and eliminating it several hours before bedtime will improve sleep. Drinking alcohol before bedtime can be a detriment to sleeping well. Although alcohol may make us drowsy initially, more often than not, alcohol will cause early awakening and unsound sleep.

What can help us improve our sleep is to start winding down from our daily activities at least an hour before our established bedtime. During this period of preparation, we can listen to calming music, read magazines or inspirational material, take a warm bath or shower, engage in gentle stretching, and practice meditation. Sometimes a sound machine with "white noise" or a similar smartphone application can lull one to sleep. If none of these strategies is effective, one should see a qualified medical professional who can assess the situation and prescribe appropriate interventions.

Finally, a little pampering goes a long way. Getting a massage or a facial, manicure or pedicure, or whatever one's budget can support can increase one's sense of physical well-being. Anything soothing can improve our physical selves. We can wrap up in a blanket, sip herbal tea or hot chocolate, light a candle, listen to relaxing music, or sit by a fire. Spending time in nature is rejuvenating. Bask in the sunshine. Go hiking. Sit by the ocean. Walk in the woods. Work in a garden. Do something creative or artistic such as painting, knitting, drawing, writing, or coloring in an adult coloring book. Being extra kind to our bodies will enable them to sustain us in the months and years ahead.

Emotional Self-Care

When we are grieving, our emotions are often like a runaway train—they are often so unpredictable that we feel unsettled and out of control. Grief triggers a range of emotions: sadness, fear, anger, anxiety, guilt, depression, confusion, helplessness, and many more. We may even experience several emotions simultaneously. Taking care of our emotional life is a means to feeling more in control and less afraid.

Keeping a journal of our feelings and experiences in the aftermath of our child's death can be a healing process and a way of both exploring and managing feelings that can be overwhelming. Writing down our feelings helps corral them in a way that ruminating about them cannot.

Talking with friends who are willing and able to be a nonjudgmental presence and sounding board can invite us to express feelings that are confusing or overpowering. Selecting people who can be a container for our strong emotions without feeling fearful or having a need to give advice can be a gift on the road toward healing. If we are feeling emotionally unstable or have coped with preexisting mental health issues, working with a professional counselor is an appropriate course of action.

Joining a grief support group such as Compassionate Friends [1] may be a way to connect with others who understand what it feels like to deal with a child's death. The common experience can provide a safe place to share feelings and to gather emotional support.

Engaging in pleasurable activities, however small, can lift our spirits in large ways. Taking a walk with a friend, going shopping, watching a sports event, going to the movies or a concert or other live entertainment can boost our mood. Consider doing something you enjoy each day. It is perfectly acceptable to give ourselves permission to experience joy and pleasure, even as we are grieving.

Social Self-Care

The death of our child can be disruptive to our social networks and relationships. First, we may not feel motivated to attend social events, and our erratic emotions may contribute to our reluctance to engage socially with others. Second, we may experience awkwardness in social settings because people are apt to feel uncomfortable talking about our child's death despite the glaring reality of it. They are unsure whether to mention our child's name or to go on acting as if nothing tragic had happened. Third, we may need time to be alone for introspection and quiet rather than to be engaged in social interaction.

At some point, however, we must reenter the world of social and familial networks and activities. One way to take care of ourselves socially is to let our friends and associates know we may not feel up to social gatherings or we may need to leave early if they become too difficult for us. Planning ahead gives us a safety valve and an escape hatch as we begin to make our way back to social activities. Another strategy is to tell our friends and family members what we need from them. We cannot expect them to read our minds. We may need to tell them it is important to us to talk about our deceased child, just as it is important for them to discuss their living children. We may need to be very direct and share the truth that others' silence in the face of our pain is not helpful or protective. Instead, it exacerbates our suffering by denying it. Also, when we feel able, it is important to tell stories about our children when the memories surface. Doing so honors our children's lives and perpetuates their memory.

Mental Self-Care

When we are reeling with grief, we are searching desperately for something—*anything*—to take away the pain and to relieve our minds from the constant processing of what happened to our child. Some "conventional wisdom" may tell us to keep busy so we won't think about our loss. But, slowing ourselves down is actually a healthier choice. Taking care of our minds and our cognitive health involves giving ourselves permission not to be perfect. We can give ourselves a break and lower our expectations during the most severe periods of our grief. We can educate others that it may take some time before we are back to our "normal" performance level. We can limit our "to do" lists and not attempt to accomplish as much every day as we did before or as we may think is required.

Another thing we can do to take care of our minds is to focus on things we are good at doing. By underscoring our strengths, we gain a sense of mastery and accomplishment that may be lacking when our thinking gets foggy and we are lost in a miasma of confusion. Maybe we are good at organizing data or ideas or things. Perhaps we are good at crossword puzzles, Sudoku, or word games. Creative endeavors such as cooking, sewing, woodworking, or tinkering remind us we have not lost our minds, but rather, we are just grieving.

Spiritual Self-Care

Taking care of our spiritual lives (if this arena is important to us) is imperative as we navigate our grief journey. Our minds bombard us with questions: "What has happened to my child's spirit?" "Is my child in 'heaven'?" "How could a loving God allow this tragedy to happen?" "How can I find meaning in my life without my child?" Reading books about spirituality and loss may also help address the nagging questions. Talking with a religious leader or spiritual director may provide an opportunity to reflect on the questions and gain insight into the troubling uncertainties.

Mindfulness

Mindfulness is a spiritual practice that involves paying attention in the present without judging ourselves. So often we move mindlessly through the activities of our day lost in thought about other people, past conversations, plans for the weekend, or dreams of a life we may have one day in our future. While we are daydreaming or reminiscing, we are unaware of what we are eating, how we are feeling, or what is going on in the moment in an interaction with another person. For example, I have had occasions of driving across town only to arrive at my destination completely unaware of how I got there. It is frightening to consider how *mindlessly* I drove through traffic paying little attention to anything except whatever thoughts and plans were running through my brain at the time. Mindfulness is a discipline we can cultivate to help us stay focused on the present, reduce our stress, slow our agitated minds, and help us manage our pain. It isn't a cure for our sorrow, but it puts us in touch with our moment-to-moment experience.

Meditation

Meditation is a form of mindfulness that involves sitting still and being quiet while we focus on our breath, a mantra, the voice of a guide, or simply clearing our minds. It is the practice of being aware of the present moment. In this stillness, we slow ourselves down and come face to face with the whisperings of our hearts. Although meditation is simple, it is not easy. We are not accustomed to a heightened focus, and our culture invites us to escape from pain and discomfort. Our minds are restless, full of chatter, and our thoughts run nonstop like the stock market ticker tape at the bottom of a television screen. Meditation is a means of calming the storm within. It requires practice, as even the basic act of following our breath finds us distracted by passing thoughts. Time and time again in meditation, we return to the breath or the object of our focus. Jack Kornfield, well-known proponent of meditation and author of *A Path With Heart*, wrote, "Meditation is very much like training a puppy. You put the puppy down and say, 'Stay.' Does the puppy listen? It gets up and it runs away. You sit the puppy back down again."[2] Kornfield describes how learning to meditate requires constant self-vigilance without judgment. As we focus on our breath or repeating a few words over and over, we acknowledge the times when our thoughts run away and we become distracted. Then we simply bring our focus back to the breath or the mantra.

Fortunately, there are many resources available in books, CDs, apps, and online to guide those seeking to deepen their spiritual lives through meditation. In addition, there are workshops, training institutes, and retreat centers specializing in teaching meditation techniques. Although learning to practice mindfulness and meditation may be difficult, the positive benefits are worth the struggle. Thus, being patient with the process of self-examination and meaning-making will also help us in our grief.

Self-Care During Holidays

Often holidays are emotionally difficult for grievers. Everything around us shouts of joy and celebration, of fun and frolic, and those are the last feelings in our hearts. Holidays evoke deep memories of years past when we were not tormented by the ravages of addiction. Holidays emphasize emptiness that can't be filled with food or festivities, by presents or pageantry. They remind us of what we have lost and how irreplaceable our child is. During holidays, we are poignantly reminded of the empty chair at the table, the empty Christmas stocking, the missing one at the table when the candles on the menorah are lit. Often we avoid the traditions we once loved as a means of minimizing the pain that seems exacerbated by the veneer of sentimentality surrounding holidays. The cruel juxtaposition of joy and sorrow elicited by the holidays can trigger depression in someone who is juggling the demands of grief fairly well on an ordinary day. Because of these challenges, making a plan for self-care during the holidays is essential.

There are several ways to be intentional about navigating the holidays well. First, we can lower our expectations. It is unrealistic to think we will ever return to the way holidays were prior to our child's death. The door to those times has closed. We can reduce the likelihood of disappointment and more sadness by not expecting things to be the same. We can make a special effort to connect with others who empathize with our loss so we can feel free to express whatever we are experiencing as we travel through those tender days. We can give ourselves permission to be selectively social and to say no to any invitations or events if the thought of them feels too overwhelming or painful. We can plan some entertainment that makes us laugh such as watching a funny movie. We can take time to nurture the ongoing connection with our child by sharing memories, talking about our children, expressing our feelings, reminiscing about ornaments, looking at old photos, or lighting a candle. We can slow ourselves down from the hustle and bustle and stress that characterize the holidays. We can make time to sit still, to spend time in nature, to meditate, to breathe, to be. In some communities, churches offer programs called

"Blue Christmas," which are focused on providing support for persons who are grieving any kind of loss during the holidays. These events may offer solace during the difficult days. Indeed, the holidays add a unique dimension to the grief experience. Taking charge of how we respond can be a means of self-care. And offering hospitality to grief, the uninvited guest, may help us move forward in new ways as we traverse the holidays.

My Self-Care Efforts

After Cameron's death, I resolved to practice as much self-care as possible, knowing it would facilitate my passage through heart-rending grief. In terms of physical self-care, I forced myself to exercise most every day. Even if I did not make it to the gym, simply taking a walk in the neighborhood gave me more energy and lifted my mood. Although I ate a fairly healthful diet prior to this loss, I began to focus on making sure I was getting the nourishment I needed. Initially, I had no interest in food. I felt nauseated at the thought of eating. But, I coerced myself to take small bites of nutritional foods throughout the day and to drink water. I eliminated caffeine almost entirely. About a year after Cameron's death, I stopped eating refined sugars and processed foods. These changes involved small steps over time and have resulted in my improved health and increased stamina.

Sleeping well has been a significant challenge in the wake of Cameron's death. Although I have worked diligently on the approaches to sleep improvement discussed above,

I continue to wrestle with sleep disruption. If I cannot get to sleep in about an hour, I get up, write down my thoughts, read something relaxing, and try sleeping in the guest room or on the sofa. I have discovered some sleep meditations and sleep stories that harness my runaway mind and help me relax. Using these strategies eventually results in my falling asleep.

Pampering has been a healing experience for me since Cameron's death. Although I winced at the expense at first, I began scheduling regular massages with a sensitive and competent practitioner. I learned I was holding much of my grief in my body, and the regular release of tension and pain was a gift to myself I have not regretted. Practicing yoga, too, has been a means of releasing tension and inviting relaxation. In addition, I have tried to spend at least some time each day outside. Being in natural settings helps me feel renewed. Every time I have an opportunity, I go to the mountains, the ocean, or forest and breathe in the calm and rejuvenating energy they offer.

Emotionally, I've been fortunate to have a circle of friends with whom I can share feelings. I've also been able to express myself through writing. And, giving myself the freedom to revel in pleasurable activities, however small, makes it possible for me to enjoy the exquisite beauty of life even while carrying the heavy, ugly mantle of grief.

Socially, I learned I preferred the company of a smaller circle of friends in the months right after Cameron's death. Although I have enjoyed lots of socializing in other periods of my life, I am content with a slower pace and with surrounding myself with people whom I know can tolerate the pain of my grief.

The mental fog that enveloped me in the first months following Cameron's death was a staunch adversary to my sense of self. I was constantly combatting my feelings of incompetence and failure when my mind would betray me. I had a difficult time forgiving myself and being more gracious with myself when I would make errors with work or simply forget to do something important. Finally, I started asking myself how I would respond to someone else who was grieving and experiencing these same mental challenges. I knew I would have given anyone else much more latitude than I offered myself. When I began to slow myself down and lower my expectations about my productivity, I noticed I began to improve cognitively.

And, as silly as it may seem, I immersed myself in online word games with like-minded friends. This activity forced me to focus mentally, reinforced my skill, kept my mind from ruminating about the details of Cameron's dreadful and untimely death, and helped me fall asleep in the wee hours of the morning after tossing and turning without relief.

I feel fortunate that I have not experienced a crisis of faith with regard to my religious and spiritual beliefs. I believe having had to address these thorny issues of faith in my theological training and in my work as a clergyperson prepared me for my own experience of the difficult questions later. Instead, I have found myself opening up to spiritual realities and practices outside of my religious and spiritual tradition. I have learned more about mindfulness and meditation and attempted to integrate them more into my life. I have been willing to consider the notion that perhaps the dead continue to communicate with us from the "other side." I have sharpened my senses and begun to trust my intuition more deeply as I embrace more and more of the mystery of life and death.

Even though several years have now passed since Cameron's death, the holidays remain difficult. Memories of holidays past flood in, and invariably I try to imagine what it would be like to have Cameron with me to celebrate once again. Sadness still creeps in when I remember making his favorite breakfast or dessert, or when I consider my Christmas tradition of writing a poem with clues about where his major gift might be. I have learned I need to simplify holidays to reduce the extra stress that grief already brings, to create new traditions and to spend time with people who truly empathize with the conundrum holidays present for those of us forever changed by loss.

Grief takes an incredible toll on every aspect of our lives: our bodies, our emotions, our relationships, our minds, our spiritual selves, and our experience of holidays and holy days. Acknowledging the degree to which we can become impaired by loss, and being willing to give ourselves time and space to practice self-care goes a long way toward helping us regain the balance necessary to carry on with our lives.

Questions for Reflection:

» How have you experienced your grief physically?
Socially? Emotionally? Mentally? Spiritually?

» How has grief manifested itself in these areas?

» What forms of self-care have your practiced?

» What other types of self-care do you think would be
helpful?

» What are the next steps in your self-care plan?

CHAPTER 5:
RESILIENCE: TO BEND BUT NOT BREAK

THE DEATH OF one's child is a loss that may seem insurmountable. When confronted with the crushing news of a child's death, it is common for parents to believe they cannot survive this excruciating loss. And, tragically, some do not. However, most people *do* survive their child's death, and on the continuum of resilience, some appear to cope with and adapt to the loss better than others do. In this chapter, I describe *resilience*, that is, how individuals and families cope with adversity and how they are able to turn the adversity into a catalyst for growth.

Trait-Based Resiliency

Some research on resiliency suggests that it involves possessing traits that predict how one will manage a crisis or a loss. A number of individual factors beyond our control including gender, age, developmental stage, and the prior relationship with the deceased may contribute to our ability to manage the death of a child. Also, there are several types of individual attributes such as social networks, financial resources, and ethnic community involvement that affect how people adapt to the tragedy of losing a child.

Nancy Hooeyman and Betty Kramer, in their book, *Living Through Loss: Interventions Across the Life Span*,[1] emphasized the fact that men and women are likely to experience and react to loss differently. Women, who are socialized to be more emotionally expressive, may cry and share their feelings of pain and despair with close friends and family members. Men, on the other hand, may refrain from expressing their emotions publicly, and instead channel the energy of their grief into funeral arrangements or lose themselves in their work. Sometimes those differences create distance in a heterosexual couple's relationship. However, despite general gender differences, a tragedy such as the loss of a child has the power to bring couples closer.

Hooeyman and Kramer also wrote about the ways age and developmental stage affect our resilience in the face of loss. Older adults tend to manage loss better than do younger ones because usually they have experienced more losses and have come to understand loss as an inevitable part of life. This fact isn't true under all circumstances, however. Those who have experienced numerous and traumatic losses may not have the inner resources to manage more loss, especially the loss of a child. Because the death of a child is not something parents expect to happen, this developmental incongruence challenges one's resilience.

Grievers' individual characteristics also signal resiliency, according to Hooeyman and Kramer. Those who are assertive, flexible, tenacious, optimistic, and able to make meaning of the loss tend to cope better than those who are not.

Although some of these characteristics may be more innate to some than to others, each can be developed. Further, those who exhibit the will to do or be something tend to be resilient. Finally, individuals who profess religious and spiritual beliefs, addressed later in chapter 7, also are associated with more resilience in coping with the death of a loved one.

In addition to the individual characteristics discussed above, Hooeyman and Kramer noted that social networks, economic resources, cultural practices, and general well-being mitigate the devastating toll grief takes on mourners. Having people to whom we can turn when we are living the nightmare of the death of a child helps tremendously in bolstering resilience. Those with access to family, friendship, religious/spiritual, and community networks seem to fare better as they navigate the rough waters of grief. However, at times, some members of these networks fail to deliver the support we need or expect. Sometimes this lack of support is the result of others (such as family members) being shattered by the same loss such that they cannot tolerate our need to talk about the loss or express our feelings about it. Doing so often results in our exacerbating their grief. Other times, members of our support networks turn out to be less supportive than we had hoped. Out of their discomfort with our grief or their confusion about what to say to comfort us, they end up saying things that are offensive or hurtful. For example, well-meaning friends and acquaintances may tell us how we "should" grieve, pronounce that our children are "in a better place," or they may suggest we "get on with our lives." Further, they may remain silent in the face of our pain, thus worsening our tendency toward social withdrawal and isolation. Because positive social support may be critical to our healing journey, if our existing social networks fail us, seeking out other forms of social support, such as grief groups, may be important.

> *"Our child dies a second time when*
> *no one speaks their name."*[2]
> - Sheryl Sandberg, *Option B*

Beyond social resources, economic resources also contribute to one's capacity for resilience. Those who are able to meet their financial obligations and are fortunate enough to have some savings and disposable income are somewhat insulated from the ongoing stress of worrying about money. Also, because the costs of death, including preparing the deceased's body and paying for the funeral, are ever increasing, being financially strapped adds to the difficulty of managing grief. Moreover, those with financial resources are better able to pay for services such as childcare, housekeeping, or eating out in restaurants that minimize some of the demands of daily living.

Another aspect of strength and resilience is embedded in the communities to which individuals belong. Participation in cultural rituals and practices may be a positive resilience factor. Ethnic and religious ways of honoring the deceased through wakes, visitation, food preparation and sharing, and funerals or memorial services bolster one's ability to cope with debilitating loss.

Our personal well-being, including low levels of anxiety and depression as well as lack of physical illness, also contributes to overall resilience. Thus, individual resilience in the face of a significant loss, such as the death of a child, is composed of mental and physical health, positive social relationships, the ability to stay connected to the deceased, and the capacity to make meaning of the loss and to build a life after loss. Ultimately, whatever is "working" that contributes to overall well-being for individuals experiencing grief can be considered resilience.

Family Resilience

While there is a long history of research on individual resilience, families, too, exhibit signs of more or less adaptation to loss based on how well they are able to fulfill their functions. The major functions of a resilient family include a sense of belonging, economic support, nurture and socialization, and protection of vulnerable members.[3]

Joan Patterson, a well-known researcher in the field of family stress and coping, developed the Family Adjustment and Adaptation Response (FAAR) model to describe how families experience and cope with stress. Patterson explained family adjustment as an interaction between the *demands* a family must manage, the *capabilities* it has to address the demands, and the meaning the family makes of its circumstances. The demands on a family include stressors, strains, and daily hassles facing the family. The capabilities to address these demands include the various resources, tangible, such as money, or intangible, such as attitudes or coping strategies. The meaning-making aspect of the model includes the family's perceptions of their demands and capabilities, that is, how they see themselves as a family.[3] The meaning-making dimension also includes the story the family tells itself about its crises and its ability to respond to them.

Families are constantly juggling their life demands and their capabilities in order to attain *family adjustment*. However, when the demands exceed the capacities, a *crisis* ensues, and the family must struggle to regain equilibrium after being thrown off balance by the crisis. When the family is able to restore balance, either through reducing demands, increasing capabilities, or changing meanings or perceptions, the outcome is good and they are said to possess *regenerative power*. If the family gets derailed and is not able to restore equilibrium in the face of a crisis, it

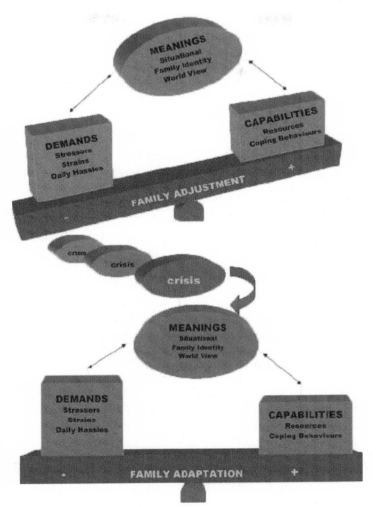

The Family Adjustment and Adaptation Response (FAAR) Model,
Patterson, 1989, p. 236 [4]

experiences poor adaptation or *vulnerability.*[5] Families are
always in flux, and thus their adjustment and adaptation to
crises are ongoing processes and not fixed traits. Therefore,
one cannot say, "We are a well-adjusted family," because

that descriptor may change over time and in relation to the types of crises each family faces and the degree to which the family responds to the demands required by the crisis.

When families face an unexpected traumatic event, such as the death of a child, this event forces the family to extreme functioning, for better or for worse. Either the family rises to manage the trauma by developing new capabilities, or it becomes overwhelmed by the demands and may experience poor adaptation.

Researchers studied 89 Belgian families after the death of a child. They found that "family strengths in general, and commitment to the family in particular, helped the families' adaptation after the loss."[6]

Patterson's work on family adaptation to stress has been a significant theoretical model in my toolbox as a therapist and educator for over 30 years. I had no way of knowing then that I would find her work on family resilience so personally meaningful. Over the weeks, months, and now years following Cameron's death, I have been able to make sense of my grief experience (crisis) in terms of how well my family members and I were able to offset stressors, demands, and hassles with resources of all kinds: financial, emotional, intellectual, cultural, social, and spiritual. And, I have been empowered by the ability to make meaning of our incredible loss in ways that undergird my faith in life and the universe rather than destroy it.

I am well aware I was born with the privilege of being White and growing up in a middle-class family with parents who valued education and gave me every opportunity to expand my world. And, they raised me in a church with a particular theology—one with which I would wrestle personally and professionally and ultimately rework and retain. I arrived in this world with numerous resources by sheer luck or grace, and most of my family members have had these same privileges. Other resources, such as social support, were the result of my long commitment to building and maintaining a large friendship network.

The demands, too, were not as huge or menacing as they could have been had Cameron's death occurred at other times in my life. I was not working full-time and going to school simultaneously, raising other children, writing a book, going through a divorce, or being a caregiver for a dying parent. When our family crisis hit, life was calm by comparison, tensions were few, and hassles were manageable.

I had learned through my own research that our perceptions shape our appraisal of our experiences. I was clear from the beginning of my grief journey that how I viewed what happened to Cameron would shape me going forward, and it would be a catalyst for either harm or healing. Cameron's death presented me with the opportunity to make sense of and create meaning from this life-altering loss.

Fostering Resilience

As heart-breaking as Cameron's death has been for me and my family members, I am poignantly aware others are traveling a rockier road with more challenges, demands and burdens than I have had to shoulder. I have, however, had times when I felt a kind of paralysis that kept me from completing all the activities and work-related tasks on my agenda. I have had periods in which I felt anxious and hyper-vigilant. I have endured days or weeks when I felt unusually self-absorbed and reluctant to engage in social interaction. All of us have broad and varied grief experiences and struggles. And I believe negotiating the path of grief calls for comradeship, not comparison.

If you are reading this book and are worried that you do not possess the traits described above or you are concerned about your family's struggles, do not despair. Fortunately, there is evidence that it is possible to develop resilience in various ways. The first approach is to consider the strengths you have accrued as you have faced other life challenges and to tap into them as resources for your grief journey. The second approach is to cultivate resilience by engaging in strategies known to help people survive a crisis and emerge stronger from it.

Tapping into Existing Strengths

On the path through adulthood, all of us face challenges, setbacks, failures, disappointments, and losses. These experiences result in the acquisition of strengths we may not realize we have. In fact, sometimes we tend to minimize our strengths and emphasize our weaknesses. Reflecting on times when we conquered difficulties or overcame obstacles can help us identify our strengths and make use of them as we strive to become more resilient. Perhaps we are effective organizers, communicators, influencers, risk-takers, analyzers, or empathizers. Maybe we have been courageous, persistent, open-minded, creative, curious, or mindful. Possibly we can point to times we have been adventurous, self-confident, motivated, energetic, hopeful, or resourceful. There are countless ways our accumulated knowledge, skills, and personal qualities can be used to foster the resilience we need to move along our grief journey.

Consider writing the answers to the following questions as a means of discovering existing individual strengths:

» When confronted with a difficulty in the past, how did you respond?
» When faced with stressful circumstances, what enabled you to maintain inner balance or calm?
» When you encountered a challenging situation, what helped you maintain perspective?
» When you have been faced with other losses, how did you cope?

Responses to the following questions can help identify family strengths:

» What are some of your family's strengths?
» What has your family taught you about how to respond to a crisis?
» How have you received emotional support from your family members in the past?

» How can your family members be helpful to you now?
» How has your family dealt successfully with challenges before?
» If your family has not been helpful to you in managing past challenges, how have you learned to cope with difficulties and build resilience?

By writing down the answers to these questions, it is possible to discover both individual and family strengths that can contribute to fostering resilience in the face of grief. Review all of the individual factors associated with resilience discussed above. Make a commitment to yourself to work on the ones that seem easiest and will be the most helpful. Examine the answers to the family-strength questions to determine how you and your family members have tackled tough times in the past. Consider ways to use family strengths to reduce stressors, demands, and hassles and to increase resources to balance out the pressure and give you more energy for dealing with loss. If your family has not been able to support you in positive ways, recall whom you relied on for emotional support and what you have learned from others about resilience.

Cultivating Strategies of Resilience

Research cited at the beginning of this chapter suggests that resilience is a static trait that is hardwired in us. We may believe that either we are resilient or we are not. Current research in neuroscience, the study of brain function, reveals that our brains can be rewired and can create new structures to help us recover from trauma. Because of *neuroplasticity* (the ability of the brain to create new capacity), the brain is by nature resilient. It can respond with flexibility, adapt to trauma, stress, and loss.[7] Today we know that we have much more ability to cultivate resilience than was previously thought.

Cultivating resilience is possible, but it takes time and practice. Just like bodybuilders don't walk into a gym on their first day of weight lifting and hoist a 200-pound barbell over their heads, we who are nurturing our resilience have to work at it a little bit day by day. In time, the bodybuilder can bench press hundreds of pounds and has the muscles to show it. As we develop our resilience and rewire our brains, eventually, over time, we will notice how strong we have become.

There are several strategies that can be employed to increase one's resiliency when facing adversity such as the death of a child. These strategies are the following:

» Reach out to others
» Be hopeful
» Nurture yourself
» Identify your purpose
» Accept change
» Restructure your thinking
» Seek a resilient role model
» Practice mindfulness
» Engage in empathy
» Embrace the imperfect

Reach Out to Others.

One of the most effective ways of becoming more resilient is to seek emotional support from family, friends, religious or spiritual leaders, and/or colleagues. If none of those people is available or able to help you, seek a support group in your community or in an online chat room. Seeking psychotherapy, too, can be a positive way of reaching out. Leaning on an existing support network or building one will increase one's ability to move along the grief path. Simply talking about the loss will make it more bearable.

Be hopeful.

Hope is the expectation or desire for certain things to happen. By becoming hopeful about our resilience, we can create it in ourselves. Refusing to believe that all is lost and that we will never be able to go on with our lives makes way for hope to take root and grow. We can ask ourselves, "What do I want my future to look like?" If we want to feel free to be happy again and to engage in enjoyable activities, we can determine what specific steps we will need to take to move toward that goal.

Hope is the thing with feathers
That perches in the soul,
And sings the tune without the words,
And never stops at all.
- Emily Dickinson

Nurture yourself.

In chapter 4, I described in detail ways to engage in self-care that can mitigate overwhelming sorrow. These practices can also build resilience. Taking care of our physical needs, including adequate nutrition, hydration, exercise, and sleep, makes us healthier and more able to manage the pain of grief. Learning to soothe ourselves through music, art, dance, poetry, writing, being outside, exploring nature, or engaging in other enjoyable activities can also increase resilience.

Identify your purpose.

A life purpose is what motivates us and organizes our life's goals. It is what keeps us going day by day. For some people, their life's purpose is connected to a vocation. For others, it revolves around family and social networks. Still others adopt a religious or spiritual purpose. Some people's life purpose involves aspects of all of these examples. When our life has meaning and purpose, we are fully engaged, feel connected, and believe we are doing what we were meant to do. Living on purpose helps us focus on the big picture while coping with the emotional difficulties a major loss hands us.

Sometimes when we experience a tragic loss, such as the death of our child through a drug overdose, our life purpose changes. We may be motivated to honor our child through working on substance abuse prevention, taking steps with others to combat addiction, organizing our communities, lobbying legislators, establishing support groups, or writing blogs. A sense of purpose keeps life crises in perspective. Finding or remembering our life purpose enables us to be more resilient in responding to loss.

Accept change.

One of the most challenging aspects of life is the fact that nothing stays the same. Everything changes: seasons, relationships, health, interests, beliefs, and routines. Major losses, such as the death of a child, cause cataclysmic change that can be overwhelming and cause us to lose our balance. Accepting change is a means of increasing our resiliency. Andrew Zolli, in his *New York Times* opinion piece, alluded to the importance of accepting change when he wrote that we must "roll with the waves instead of trying to stop the ocean."[8]

> *"It is not the most intellectual of the species that survives; it is not the strongest that survives; but the species that survives is the one that is able best to adapt and adjust to the changing environment in which it finds itself."*
> - Leon Megginson[9]

Restructure your thinking.

The cognitive-behavioral school of psychotherapy is known for the theory that our *thoughts* drive our feelings and our behaviors. If we change our thoughts, we will see change in our feelings and our actions. Through the process of *reframing* we can change our self-defeating thoughts by consciously inserting more positive ones. We can look at situations from a slightly different perspective. A kaleidoscope is a good example of reframing. When one holds a kaleidoscope up to the light, even the slightest turn of the tube results in a totally different pattern.

When we perceive our circumstances as a threat, our body's fear response is activated and it releases hormones that increase our blood pressure and result in more anxiety. Conversely, when we consider our situation as a challenge, our body releases hormones for cell repair, relaxation, and efficient energy usage.[10] Changing our thinking is a powerful tool for building resilience.

Seek a resilient role model.
We all know people who appear to be more resilient than we are. We can study people we admire who are resilient. We can analyze how they deal with adversity and then imitate them.[11] Role models do not have to be people we know personally. They can be historical figures, celebrities, sports heroes, political officials, or anyone who exhibits resilience. Reading the biographies of people famous for overcoming challenges can help us understand what they did to deal with their distress. We can learn about their lives and implement the strategies they used when faced with losses or tragedies.

Practice mindfulness.

As mentioned earlier, mindfulness is a practice based on the Buddhist contemplative tradition. It involves the nonjudgmental awareness and acceptance of experience. The increase in self-awareness allows us to observe what is happening and to note our reactions to it. When we are mindful of our surroundings and our experience, we are able to respond to crises with more flexibility. When we engage in mindfulness, we understand intimately what impermanence means: that this, too, shall pass. When we are mindful, we can imagine different ways of responding to our circumstances. Mindfulness can aid in the rewiring of our brain and is one of the most powerful means of cultivating resilience.[12] (See *Appendix A* for a list of resources to aid in the development of mindfulness)

Engage in empathy.

Empathy involves being attuned to our own and others' inner experience and emotions. It means imagining how people feel with the intent to understand and accept the meaning of their experience. Empathy elicits compassion for others that results in caring about their suffering. Empathy includes acceptance of what *is* so it is possible to move along in life. Being empathic toward ourselves means we are able to be compassionate and self-accepting of all the parts of ourselves, including the ways we have experienced suffering and loss.

Sometimes when I find myself being impatient with the more intense moments of grief and sadness, I ask myself,

"How would you respond to another person who was experiencing this type of emotional pain?" Immediately I know I would be much more understanding and gracious with another than I am with myself. I would encourage another person suffering with grief pangs to accept these moments as part of the process. Being intentional about cultivating self-empathy is a helpful approach to building resilience. Such empathy enables us to access our inner resources and improves our ability to cope with challenges. Empathy is the cornerstone of resilience.

Embrace imperfection.

Leonard Koren wrote about the Japanese concept of Wabi-Sabi.[13] It means to find beauty in things that are imperfect, impermanent, and incomplete. It is a philosophy that contradicts the Western focus on what is perfect, enduring, and monumental.[13] Our significant losses underscore these truths about how much of life is imperfect, impermanent and incomplete. Rather than pushing back against the brokenness, this Japanese philosophy invites us to discover the beauty in our imperfect, impermanent, incomplete lives. When we can embrace these aspects of life, we increase our aptitude for resilience.

In the months and years since Cameron's death, I have worked to become resilient. Some of these practices come easily to me. It is natural for me to reach out to others for support. I have a sturdy hopefulness and an unwavering sense of purpose. I am intentional about nurturing myself and make every effort to eat well, exercise and get enough sleep. I try to monitor my thinking, and when I realize I am entertaining negative thoughts, I remind myself I have the power to change those thoughts from negative to positive. I make every effort to be open to change and to seek resilience in others who inspire me. As a counselor, I have spent decades honing the skill of empathy for others. My challenge now is to offer that same empathy to myself that I am quick to offer to others.

In this grief journey, my ordeals have been in the areas of practicing mindfulness and embracing imperfection. I have struggled to stay present to what I am experiencing and feeling. My untamed mind wanders back to both pleasant and terrible memories. It fast-forwards ahead to plans, hopes, and fears about the future. My mind is always busy; it is rarely still. Committing to a mindfulness practice has been a tremendous challenge and a grounding experience. The calm that emerges from training my mind to stay present is a welcomed gift.

Celebration of the imperfect, the impermanent, and the incomplete is contrary to a lifetime spent striving for perfection, holding tightly to all I cherish lest it slip away, and always finishing what I start. Learning to embrace the beauty in the imperfect and incomplete simultaneously pushes my limits and opens me to new possibilities and binds me to others. Being willing to open my clenched fists and let go of everything I want to hold on to forever is paradoxically frightening and liberating.

In summary, when we are resilient, we are like palm

trees that do not snap in a storm. Instead, they bend under a strong wind and then bounce back. The individual and family-related factors described above contribute to our flexibility and resilience. And, even if we do not possess all of these attributes, the good news is that in the aftermath of a great loss we can cultivate increased resilience by relying on past strengths and implementing a variety of effective practices. Some practices are easier than others. All of them increase our hardiness and help us to bend rather than break.

QUESTIONS FOR REFLECTION:

» How do you see yourself as resilient?

» What specific characteristics of resilience do you possess?

» In what ways have you tried to cultivate resilience?

» Who are your role models of resilience? What have they done to cope with personal challenges or loss?

» What new approaches to building resilience can you begin to add to your repertoire?

CHAPTER 6:
BEING STUCK: WHEN YOU CAN'T SEEM TO MOVE ALONG IN YOUR LIFE

ALL OF US who experience the death of a child are plunged into the depths of grief. We feel sadness; we may have sleep and appetite disruptions; we wander in a mental fog; we can't concentrate; we have difficulty remembering things; we find going to work and staying focused almost impossible; we can't imagine how we will ever go on; and we wish we could turn back the clock and do something to prevent this horrific loss. Sometimes these symptoms persist for many months and even beyond the first anniversary of our child's death. The types of grief experiences are similar among mourners, though there are individual differences in the length and severity of these aspects of grief. Eventually, the majority of us are able to pick up the pieces of our lives, return to full or nearly full functioning, make some kind of sense of the tragic death of our child, and reenter the world of work, family life, social engagement, and community involvement. Somehow, most of us are able to reach into ourselves and access the deep well of resilience we may not have realized was there. We find ourselves blazing a trail where there was none and discovering personal transformation in the process.

And then there are others, between 2.4% and 4.8% of us, and perhaps even more,[1] whose symptoms persist and worsen, who don't get back on track, who are preoccupied with their child's death, entertain suicidal thoughts, who are unable to stop ruminating about their loss, and who experience poorer physical and mental health. They are experiencing *Persistent Complex Bereavement,*[2] a mental health diagnosis made for those whose intense, unrelenting grief responses interfere with their ability to carry on with their lives.

Signs of Being "Stuck" in Unrelenting Grief

If our child's death was particularly traumatic, and if we were witness to that trauma, our grief process may be more complicated than if trauma were not involved. One could say that the death of a child is, by nature, traumatic, and it is certainly off-time; however, there are some specific symptoms that characterize trauma. Stephen Fleming wrote that some grievers reexperience the trauma, attempt to avoid it, undergo a kind of emotional numbing, and are subject to hyper-arousal. In reexperiencing trauma, Fleming noted that the bereaved may have intrusive thoughts, dreams, or nightmares when reminded of the death. Avoiding and numbing behaviors and feelings include distancing from anything that calls up the memory of the deceased, not engaging in formerly pleasurable activities, feeling cut off from others, experiencing a limited range of emotions, and not being able to imagine a positive future going forward. Hyper-arousal includes sleep disruption; being constantly vigilant; feeling agitated, angry or irritable; having trouble concentrating and startling easily.[3] This layer of trauma surrounding grief may contribute to the persistence and intensity of grief and interfere with the ability to recalibrate one's life and move forward.

As I read about persistent complex bereavement and trauma, I felt grateful that a year after Cameron's death I had not found myself sinking into the quagmire of overwhelming grief that prevented me from picking up the pieces of my heart and going about my "new" life. Most certainly, I had moments when I experienced longing and deep sorrow for a son who would never finish college nor succeed in some life's work, would never get married or have children. As my peers' adult children were moving through predictable life transitions and passages, I ached that my child's future was cut short by his enslavement to heroin. I mourned for the relationship with grandchildren that would never be, and despaired at my accumulation of photo albums, precious family mementos and hard-earned financial resources that would never have an heir. But this sadness did not crush me. Instead, it punctuated my experiences and reminded me that "grief is the price we pay for loving."[4]

In addition, there were moments of self-blame, wondering how I could have missed the obvious signs of addiction early enough to insist on rehab, or why I hadn't stopped enabling and rescuing Cameron sooner than I did. But these self-blaming thoughts emerged in brief passing moments and were not an entrenched belief system that paralyzed me.

And, yes, I've been angry about Cameron's premature death from opiates. I've railed at the easy access to Oxycontin, the cheap cost of heroin, the peers and the pain that drove Cameron to use in the first place. Again, the anger has ignited in short bursts of flame when I am struck by how much of Cameron's addiction was influenced by factors outside my control. But, the anger is not a wildfire that rages for years and ultimately destroys me. It is a momentary spark or flame that flares and ultimately burns out rather swiftly.

Yes, I've felt diminished by Cameron's death. What mother wouldn't feel some loss of identity with the loss of her only child? Fortunately, through my career, my other relationships, and my hobbies, I have cultivated a strong sense of self apart from my role as a parent. However, during the times when I meet someone new and am faced with the inevitable question, "Do you have children?" I feel confused and diminished, not knowing exactly how to answer. On one hand, I know I still *have* a son, though he has departed from this life. On the other hand, I *no longer have* a child precisely because he has departed from this life. At times, this painful reality makes me feel inferior to others. And, the question about whether or not I have children makes me feel awkward because I don't want to begin a relationship having to introduce my loss in the first few moments that I encounter a new person. This experience is unsettling at best and emotionally triggering as well, but fundamentally it does not alter or eradicate my identity separate from my son.

Though the death of any child is a traumatic event for parents, I was spared some of the initial trauma surrounding Cameron's drug-overdose death because I was living 2000 miles away when it occurred. I did not find him writhing on a cold garage floor struggling to breathe. I was not called to the hospital in the night to identify him. I did not have to witness his being connected to tubes and monitors and being kept alive by machines. I did not have to tell the doctors to remove the life support. I did not have to stand next to a hospital bed and literally watch my son die. Given my distance from witnessing the actual torment, my level of trauma was not as severe as that experienced by many parents when one of their children dies from a heroin overdose. Nevertheless, I have had moments when I have felt numb and when I have wanted to avoid anything that reminds me of Cameron. I have had a few dreams where Cameron appeared, but they were not intrusive and distressing. On the contrary, they were comforting. I have had plenty of sleep-disturbed nights that still persist even four years beyond Cameron's death. But a key factor in assessing trauma is whether or not it disrupts one's ability to function at home or at work or to engage in pleasurable relationships and activities. The central question here is whether or not trauma is interfering with moving through the grief process and reclaiming one's life.

Other Signs of Prolonged and Difficult Grief

Alan Wolfelt wrote about other behavioral signs that may indicate one is "stuck" in the acute stage of grief and not able to wring oneself from its grasp. He indicated that postponement, displacement, or replacement were such signals. It is perfectly normal to find the death of one's child literally "unbelievable" or "incredible" when we first learn about it. In fact, not being able to believe our child is gone is extremely common. Even as the months and years pass, we all have moments when we want to pinch ourselves because we simply can't fathom our loss. We want someone to wake us up from this terrible, unrelenting nightmare. And, then, just as quickly, we remember we are living with this loss and it is, indeed, a fact. There are, however, those who have extreme difficulty coming to terms with the death of their child. They steel themselves against the pain. They cut themselves off from their feelings. They force back the tears. They refuse to think about it, hoping it will go away. This type of long-term denial interferes with a healthy grief process and keeps a parent from gaining the traction needed to rebuild a life.

Sometimes the pain of our loss is so intense we do not believe we can bear it, and thus, we attempt to rid ourselves of it by directing it toward other things. We lash out at family members, friends, and co-workers. We blame God. We feel angry, cynical, and hateful toward anything that potentially could bring comfort, solace, or pleasure. Essentially, this displacement of grief is the attempt to get rid of it with the hope of relieving ourselves of the pain it produces. Unfortunately, displacement only results in paralysis and disruption of the very aspects of life that could bring us some measure of healing.

Replacement of our grief is another sign we have gotten off course in our grief journey. Replacing our grief involves investing the emotions we felt in our relationship with our deceased child into someone or something else. If we are single, we may rush into a new romantic relationship, or if partnered, we may become vulnerable to an extramarital affair. We may consider having or adopting another child. Replacing our grief may mean we pour all our energy into our work or become obsessed with a particular hobby when we did not behave with that kind of intensity prior to our child's death. Although focusing on work or hobbies can bring meaning to our lives, in this instance, replacing grief means getting lost in activities in order to avoid coming to terms with the loss. Attempting to bypass the painful process of grief will likely create difficulties in the future as the unresolved grief eventually begins to corrode our relationships and our new passionate interests.[4]

Who is at Risk for Getting "Stuck"?
Although anyone who suffers from the death of a loved one may be vulnerable to persistent complex bereavement,

research results indicate certain factors such as the circumstances of the death, relationship to the deceased, access to social support, mental health status, and the degree of preventability of the death are related to how much impairment the bereaved suffer after a loss.[5] The risk of experiencing this prolonged bereavement is greater for those with mental health problems prior to the loss, those who experience other life stressors, and those who perceive that they do not have much emotional support from others. Not surprisingly, prolonged bereavement is often high among bereaved parents who have lost a child.[6]

How is Persistent Complex Bereavement Different From Depression?

Even though persistent complex bereavement and depression may appear to be similar, there are some important differences. When one is grieving intensely, the primary feelings are emptiness and loss, whereas with depression the person can't imagine ever being happy or experiencing pleasure again. Also, the sadness associated with grief is likely to wax and wane over days and weeks and to be connected to thoughts and reminders of the deceased. Depression, on the other hand, is more enduring, unspecific, and pervasive. Grievers usually retain their self-esteem; however, those who are depressed often feel worthless. If grievers do engage in self-blame, it is usually tied to feeling guilty for not doing more for the deceased or failing that person in some way.[7]

Sometimes grief and depression collide in individuals, compounding their pain and undermining their emotional stability. When this unfortunate situation occurs, the symptoms associated with grief are more debilitating and enduring than with grief alone. Although most anyone grieving could benefit from the services of a grief counselor, those who experience the intersection of grief and major depression should seek the services of a mental health professional.

Staying in a Support Group Too Long

Grief support groups can be a balm for a broken heart. Being involved with a group of people who have also lost a child and have survived this devastating, life-altering tragedy gives us companionship with others who truly understand our loss. In fact, some grievers would say their grief support groups literally saved their lives. Unfortunately, there are times when too much of a good thing becomes a bad thing. Such is the case when one stays in a support group for too long. Overstaying in a support group potentially can keep one "stuck" in the grief process, riding the tilt-a-whirl of sorrow as new members arrive bearing their gut-wrenching pain. Just as we begin to feel strong enough to carry on and to venture into an unknown future without our child, we can slide back into the pit of despair as we listen to yet another story of the death of someone's precious child. Staying too long in a support group can be like reopening a scab on a freshly healed wound. When that happens, it is probably time to move beyond the group, though staying in touch with long-time group members may be beneficial.

Not too long after Cameron's death, I considered a grief support group, but I could not seem to get there. Either I had schedule conflicts or the group was too far from my home, or I was out of town. Instead, I explored websites, read articles and books about the death of a child as I sought solace and assurance that I was eventually going to be okay. One of the most disturbing aspects of my search for information and support was my discovery of several women writing about the deaths of their children. What struck me was the fact that many of the deaths had occurred several years before, and these mothers were still devastated and somewhat debilitated by the loss. Somehow what had begun as grief support had become a lifestyle. I had to stop reading these materials because I did not want to spend the rest of my days as a servant to sorrow. Continuing to read such resources, much like staying in a support group too long, may signal one is "stuck" in the grief process.

Grief as Loyalty to the Deceased

My engagement with the grievers described above made me realize that sometimes grievers cannot move forward with their lives, not because of persistent complex bereavement or major depression but because they view their grief as a badge of loyalty they wear to honor their deceased child. They believe that if they allow themselves to integrate the loss, to engage in pleasurable activities, to rebuild their social and family relationships, to move into their "new normal" with optimism and hope, they are somehow disgracing the memory of their child and severing the bond.

Therese Rando, a well-regarded expert in grief and loss, noted that staying in pain, then, becomes a witness to one's love; therefore, moving forward would be considered betrayal of that love. She suggested that if grievers were "stuck" they could ask themselves what it would mean if they were okay and how they could move forward in their lives without losing their connection to their child.[8]

I have been blessed not to have the tendency toward depression, to have enjoyed strong physical and mental health, to have only moderate stressors, to have enjoyed far-reaching social support, and to have above average economic stability. I realize these protective factors have insulated me from some of the most egregious aspects of grief and the debilitating plague of depression.

Despite my good fortune, I had to ask myself if it was okay to be okay and to carry on with plans for celebrating my 60th birthday only three weeks after Cameron's death. Part of me felt like celebrating anything in the wake of such a tragic loss was simply wrong. I wondered if it wouldn't be more appropriate to wear the garments of mourning and let my birthday pass unobserved. The other part of me believed in celebrating life, not focusing on death. In my final deliberations, I decided to go ahead and enjoy my birthday. I think that's what Cameron would have wanted me to do.

I am well aware that not everyone has been as fortunate as I have to be able to cope reasonably well with the tragic death of my son. However, if one feels "stuck" in the grief process and is experiencing the symptoms described in this chapter or continues to wrestle with significant guilt, suicidal thoughts, extreme hopelessness, ongoing depression, physical symptoms, uncontrolled rage, impairment in social or work settings, or substance abuse, it is time to seek professional counseling from a licensed expert who can assist in addressing these issues.

How to Find a Good Grief Counselor

If you think you need professional help to move forward in your grief journey, consider asking for a referral from someone you trust who believes a particular counselor would work well with you. If you have mental health services provisions through your health insurance, you may be required to see someone who is on a preferred provider list. If that is the case, consider exploring the approved counselors' websites to determine if they have training and experience in working with bereavement, particularly with child loss. Some counselors have a certification from the Association for Death Education and Counseling (www.adec.org) that indicates specialized training. Check this website for a member directory.

Having spent many years in the mental health field training counselors, working with clients in private practice, and being a client myself, I know that not every counselor is appropriate for every client. Beyond knowledge and skills, there must be good chemistry between the counselor and the client. It is important to believe it is a good match. In order to find the best counselor, you may need to interview potential counselors either by phone or in person. Some will offer a free hour for an initial consultation to help you determine if the "fit" is good. When conducting the interviews, ask about the counselors' credentials, where they were trained, and if they specialize in bereavement counseling. It can be helpful to ask how they understand the grief process, what their approach will be, and how you will know when you are ready to terminate the counseling relationship. Once you have found a counselor, you can assess whether or not the counselor is good for you. Usually it takes a few sessions to build the relationship and to begin moving forward positively. You want to feel the counselor is trustworthy, understands you, makes sense to you, and is flexible and open to your experience and perspective on your grief journey rather than imposing a belief system on you. If you feel "out of sync" with the counselor, then it may be appropriate to seek a new one.

When we find ourselves "stuck" in the grief process, unable to move forward with our lives, it is important to look closely at our symptoms, determine if we are experiencing persistent complex bereavement, depression, or both. Or if we are trapped in the quicksand of an unhelpful support group or are maintaining the pain of our loss as a sign of our love for and loyalty to our child, then we need to seek professional help. I believe we can best love and honor our deceased children when we make space for positive memories of them and commit ourselves to a full life and an open future.

CHAPTER 7:
MAKING SENSE OF OUR CHILD'S DEATH

GIVEN THE TRAUMATIC nature of a child's death, as in a heroin overdose, it is no wonder bereaved parents often experience a cataclysmic fracture of their worldviews and their belief that life has meaning. When our child dies, suddenly our world is turned upside down. The assumptions we long held about how life was "supposed to be" seem forever dashed. The untimely death of our child calls into question who we are, what our life means now and what we will leave behind. Most of us also must come to terms with the question about the purpose of our deceased child's life. Bereavement experts have found that parents who sought to discover meaning in their loss and to restore purpose to their lives tended to fare better in the intensity of their grief and in their adjustment to life without their child than those who contended that life and loss had no meaning.[1]

*"A central task in grieving is to engage in
the process whereby one reconstructs life's
meaning in response to loss."*
- Robert A. Neimeyer
Meaning Construction and the Experience of Loss[2]

Robert Neimeyer, a well-regarded scholar on the subject of grief, noted that from the time we emerge from the initial shock of our child's death, most of us begin to try to make sense of what happened. We begin to tell a story about the tragedy and try to untangle the difficult questions about why we lost our child and what this loss means. Neimeyer contended that *meaning-making* appears as two distinct dimensions: *sense-making* and *benefit-finding*.[3] Sense-making refers to using one's view of the world and beliefs to explain the loss. Benefit-finding refers to the ways one sees positive outcomes in the aftermath of a crisis. Although it may seem odd or even impossible to find benefit in the loss of one's child, bereaved parents may discover positive opportunities and experiences arise from the ashes of loss. Grievers often find meaning in religion and spirituality and find benefits in increased compassion for others' suffering. Research suggests grieving parents who were able to make meaning of their loss experienced less mental distress, increased marital satisfaction, and improved physical health.[4]

Why Did This Loss Happen?

When we are overwhelmed with a crisis that upends the security and predictability of the world as we have known it, it is human nature to ask, "Why?" We tell ourselves that if we just understood *why* this loss occurred, perhaps we would have an easier time accepting it.

As a parent of a child whose death was the result of a heroin overdose, I have constructed some responses to the *why* questions that have enabled me to make better sense of Cameron's death and to move forward on the journey of integrating this terrible loss into life as I now know it. "Why did Cameron die of a drug overdose?" I believe some of the answers to this question lie in genetics, biology, chemistry, and psychology. Other answers are related to local environmental circumstances. Still other answers lie in Cameron's choices and behaviors. Perhaps the most astonishing answers reside in the systemic and cultural realities of our time that created the larger context for what inevitably led to Cameron's death from a heroin overdose.

As I pondered this unrelenting question of "Why?" the first responses came quickly and with a shaming vengeance as I have noted in previous chapters. Automatically, I started blaming myself. I thought, "I should have caught this sooner. I should have done more to intervene. I should have insisted on more rehab. I should have set firmer boundaries. I should not have rescued and enabled him so much. I should not have made excuses for his behavior. I have failed as a parent." Needless to say, this self-talk was not helpful. Yes, I could have done things differently, and in this horrific rearview mirror known as hindsight, I would have. But, I was not a failure as a parent. I was not perfect. But, like other parents, we did the best we could at the time. To presume Cameron's tragic death was my fault is not an adequate answer to my *why* question. It certainly does not enhance making meaning of his death. Below, I explore some of the concrete responses to the constant question, "Why?"

Genetics

Cameron was adopted at birth. We brought him home from the hospital 24 hours after the legal paperwork had been signed. In the four months before his birth, we gleaned some information about his family history and background. Some of the details were sketchy. I remember being told there was clearly a history of substance abuse in his biological family. The social worker suspected his birth father was an alcoholic. We never knew for certain the validity of this information, nor did we ever learn the extent of his biological family's substance abuse history. However, we were intentional in making Cameron aware of his potential predisposition toward substance abuse. We began these conversations when he was a preteen and continued them into his adolescence. Despite our warnings and best attempts at vigilance, Cameron started smoking cigarettes at 14. It was not a big leap for him from cigarettes to marijuana.

What I have discovered in the 30+ years hence is that

some degree of hereditability contributes to vulnerability to addictive disease. Further, genes may contribute to personality traits such as impulsivity, risk-taking, and response to stress, all of which relate to drug use and abuse.[5] Some genetic factors may also explain why some people are more vulnerable to certain drug types, especially opiates.[6] Genetic research is a complex scientific discipline and is ever-evolving as more information is discovered about the degree of genetic predisposition to drug abuse and addiction. Based on what is known currently, it seems plausible that Cameron carried genes that made him especially vulnerable to addiction.

Biology

Although it may appear genetics and biology are the same, genetics is considered a field of biology. Biology is the study of living organisms. As such, it too offers a partial explanation for Cameron's drug abuse and addiction. Researchers[7] have determined that chronic exposure to frequently abused drugs actually creates changes in the brain, including changes in expression of genes and their functioning. Specifically, substance abuse in adolescents has been associated with changes in brain structure, function, and cognition. Changes occur in brain volume, structure, and neurochemistry during adolescence. Deficits in attention, memory, and executive functioning are apparent in adolescent substance users and are associated with structural changes in the brain.[8]

Neuroscience, too, is especially complex, and new

discoveries are being made rapidly. Neuroscientists have found that the human brain is not fully developed until at least age 25 and that development can be stunted by the use of tobacco, alcohol, and drugs. What is striking to me is that Cameron's brain was nowhere near fully developed when he began using substances. Not only did the substance use and later abuse affect his brain development, it interfered with the very functions needed for him to make good decisions and take charge of his life. In Cameron's case, at least on one level, biology was destiny. The biology of brain development collided with the biology of substances resulting in a fatal outcome.

Chemistry

When Cameron began using opiates, first OxyContin and then heroin, he became a slave to the morphine molecule, entrapped for the rest of his life by the chemical laws of the drug.

Heroin is an opiate, derived from the poppy plant. When smoked or snorted or injected, opioids bind to opiate-specific receptors within the brain and decrease the body's perception of pain. They also elevate mood by greatly increasing levels of dopamine, creating intense euphoria.[9] Heroin use engulfs the body with dopamine levels much higher than those the body produces naturally for pain relief or pleasure.[10] In fact, some researchers estimate heroin use can increase the body's dopamine up to 10 times the normal level.[11] After regular opioid use and dopamine elevation, individuals begin to build tolerance to heroin. Very soon after heroin use begins, perhaps even after the first exposure, pain-signaling pathways may become overactive so the user needs increased amounts of heroin just to feel "normal." Long-term heroin use, then, affects memory, decision-making, complex thought, and control of one's own behavior.

Organic chemistry is one explanation of why Cameron died from a heroin overdose. A toxic level of heroin depresses the respiratory system, slowing down breathing significantly, and ultimately leading to respiratory arrest. High levels of heroin also affect heart rate and rhythm, interfering with the heart's ability to provide an adequate blood supply to the brain and other organs. Cardiac arrest can result. A toxic level of heroin led to Cameron's respiratory failure. The facts of brain chemistry are one reason Cameron's life was cut short.

Psychology

Cameron was a happy, fun-loving, delightful child who appeared not to have a care in the world. Our move from Florida to Colorado when he was 6 was a very difficult transition for him. We never dreamed a child so young would feel so angry and sad about leaving his familiar surroundings and playmates. But he did. Although he had tested in the "gifted" range, by second grade he was struggling in school. By late elementary school, he was diagnosed with Attention Deficit Disorder and prescribed Ritalin. He gained weight his first year in middle school and became the target of school bullies.

All of these challenges created emotional distress for him and affected his self-esteem.

By far the biggest psychological issue for Cameron was coming to terms with his adoption. Though we did not discuss it often, I am convinced Cameron's separation from his birth mother caused an emotional wound that never healed. Despite all of the love, educational opportunities, church involvement, travel, and material things we offered him, he could never rid himself of feeling utterly worthless. I believe the psychic pain of early abandonment and rejection made him unable to receive the extraordinary love offered him by family and friends. It follows, then, that he would be highly susceptible to drugs that offered him extreme pleasure and numbed the terrific pain he worked so hard to conceal.

Environmental Factors

We never could have imagined that our move to an upper-middle class neighborhood in a Denver suburb would have placed Cameron at such risk for substance abuse. Purchasing a home in that neighborhood was a financial stretch for us, and we made it work because the schools were excellent. We had no way of knowing that we were living near families whose children would become Cameron's friends and substance abusers as well. I believe peer pressure was a major reason Cameron started smoking and using drugs.

Cameron's high school, too, was saturated with drug use. It boasted an "open campus" where students could come and go during their "free" periods. In fact, the school building was not large enough to accommodate the entire student body at one time. The lax attitude toward skipping classes and using substances created an environment that made it easy for Cameron to use. Eventually, we transferred him to a smaller, more restrictive high school; however, that did little to influence his habits. Instead, he enrolled in a work-study program that afforded him the freedom to leave school and spend several hours a day at work in a fast food restaurant. That environment, too, was composed of peers whom we later learned were substance users. We assumed naively that Cameron's positive environment would protect him from access to drugs. We learned subsequently that adolescents in middle and upper-middle-class neighborhoods obtain drugs easily because they have money. Paradoxically, the environments we selected intentionally because of their positive qualities turned out to be Cameron's nemesis.

Choice and Behaviors

When I continue to ask why Cameron died from a heroin overdose, I cannot overlook the reality of his own choices and behaviors. Yes, he was genetically predisposed to substance abuse. Yes, there were biological and chemical consequences of using heroin. Yes, he was psychologically vulnerable to drug abuse as a means of managing his emotional pain. Yes, he was raised in a neighborhood and attended schools where drug use was rampant. Yes, he was highly susceptible to peer influence. And, yes, he was also responsible for decisions he made regarding friends, activities, and substance use. Unfortunately, his early decisions to use drugs affected his developing brain, which, in turn, compromised his decision-making ability and interrupted his capacity for controlling his behavior. Sadly, Cameron's compromised ability to make healthful choices ended up costing him his life.

Systemic Factors: The "Perfect Storm"

The contributing factors to Cameron's death by heroin described above might have been enough to answer the question, "Why did this happen to my son?" until I read Sam Quinones' award winning book, *Dreamland: The True Tale of America's Opiate Epidemic.*[12] In this fascinating book, Quinones, a journalist and investigative reporter, recounted how a confluence of factors over the past two decades converged to create the opioid epidemic in the United States. Quinones revealed these factors that created this "perfect storm":

» an organized network of Mexican farm boys who, in search of Levi's 501 jeans and a better life, became heroin traffickers in cities all over the U. S.;

» a misused paragraph by a Boston physician published in a medical journal minimizing the addictiveness of opiates;

» Pharmaceutical companies' development and aggressive marketing of opiate-based prescription pain killers;

» the focus on pain management and the emergence of pain clinics turned "pill mills" where pain medication was prescribed liberally;

» the low cost of Mexican "black tar" heroin that lured prescription opiate users to switch to heroin;

» the burgeoning heroin market among White suburban youth with cars and financial resources to support a heroin addiction;

» the easy access to heroin provided by Mexican "drivers" who delivered heroin like pizza to middle and upper-middle-class White suburban neighborhoods; and

» middle class parents' misperception of heroin addiction as a seedy habit that occurred among the urban poor in dilapidated housing projects.

All these factors united to create a heroin epidemic in the U.S. Indeed, more Americans died of drug overdoses in 2016 than died in the entirety of the Vietnam War.[13]

Thus, in unsuspecting middle-class neighborhoods across the United States, the heroin epidemic was exploding. It was happening all around us, and most of us were completely unaware of it. In *Dreamland*, Quinones provided another answer as to why Cameron died from a heroin overdose: he was swept up in a systemic confluence of factors that created the "perfect storm" and led inevitably to his death.

The challenge for any parent who has lost a child to heroin (or any other cause) is to make meaning of the loss. Part of that meaning-making is to wrestle with the question, "Why did this happen?" I have attempted to answer that question for myself. At the beginning of my quest, I could not help blaming myself, our decisions as parents, our divorce (which occurred long after Cameron's substance abuse began), and a myriad of other individual and parental decisions we made along the way. Now, I am convinced Cameron's death was the result of a variety of factors, most of them significantly more powerful and influential than whatever missteps we may have made as parents. As a result, I have been able to release most of the self-blame and inevitable guilt that comes with such a tragic loss.

Making Meaning and Religious and Spiritual Beliefs

A significant loss such as the death of a child invariably causes us to consider our religious and spiritual traditions and beliefs, and even lean on them, as we attempt to make meaning of our loss. As someone who hails from a western Christian tradition, my ideas have been shaped by that milieu. And given the diversity of spiritual perspectives and practices, I am acutely aware that spirituality means different things to different people. For me, spirituality is concerned with persons' search for meaning, purpose, and value in life. It may or may not include a supreme being or a higher power. Religion, on the other hand, tends to be expressed in external, organizational, behavioral, ritualistic, and public ways. Under the best of circumstances, religion is a vessel of spirituality, but not always. Because spirituality, by definition, is concerned with making meaning, naturally it plays an important role in coming to terms with loss.

When faced with the question of "Why did this happen?" it is not surprising that many people turn immediately to a spiritual or religious response. Those of Judeo-Christian background and others may claim, "It was God's will." In fact, God's will is one of the most common explanations people give when faced with the death of a loved one, even a child. People who hold this belief rely on the notion that whatever happens is part of God's perfect plan. They need not understand this plan, but rather, they take it on faith. Although undoubtedly some people find comfort and meaning in this religious response, many others find themselves lashing out in anger at God for "willing" the untimely death of their child and their own subsequent suffering. The fact that so many people view God or a higher power as an active player in their child's death suggests the need to explore our beliefs and assumptions about who God is and how God acts.

The Problem of Theodicy

If the idea that our child's death was "God's will" does not bring comfort, then it likely leads us down the path of what, in theological terms, is called "theodicy." That is, how can a good God "allow" bad things to happen, especially to "good" people? Volumes have been written about this so-called "problem of evil," and understanding all its facets requires considerable knowledge of both theology and philosophy. Nevertheless, it is important to address the basic issues raised by evil and suffering in the world because so many of us are caught in a kind of theological double jeopardy: we have lost our child *and* our faith.

Theodicy is the attempt to defend the existence of God in the face of evil and suffering. It causes us to raise questions about the characteristics of a God who either permits evil and suffering or is powerless to stop it. Typically, we assume God is all-knowing, all-powerful, and good. And we believe it is God's nature to want to destroy evil. However, if God is good, but does not prevent evil and suffering, perhaps that God is not as powerful as we had once believed. Or, perhaps if God is all-powerful and still does not prevent evil and suffering, then perhaps God is not good after all. Perhaps God is cruel instead. These explanations are not particularly comforting. If we want to hold on to the concept of a God who is good, all-powerful and all-knowing, then we may be driven to find a response for why there is evil and suffering in the world. There are no "right" answers to this dilemma; however, if we carry with us the least bit of theistic religious teaching or any shred of faith, the process of making sense of our loss may require us to delve deeply into this universal question.

Phillip Mitchell, in his "Theodicy Overview,"[14] described some of the ways people from western, monotheistic religions have come to terms with the problem of theodicy. According to Mitchell, some of the most common responses are free will, virtue development, eschatological hope, and the limits of human understanding and mystery.

Free will

The notion of free will suggests that God created humans with the freedom to choose how they behave. A God who intervenes constantly would function as the Divine Puppeteer, controlling our actions and compromising our freedom. Evil and suffering, therefore, are unfortunate consequences of humans' freedom to choose, even to choose to hurt themselves or others. Thus, God purposefully limits God's own power in order for us to own the freedom of being human. This belief leads us to see our loss as the result of all of the choices made that led our child to drug use and abuse, addiction, and finally death.

Virtue development

Essentially, this explanation suggests evil is necessary in order for us to develop virtues such as compassion, endurance, and courage in the face of pain and suffering. Leslie Weatherhead, author of the classic book, *The Will of God,* wrote, "Evil is never creative of good, though the circumstances of evil have often been an occasion for the expression of good."[15] This explanation means loss is good for us in some way, and it will make us stronger. Those who hold this view often believe that our life is one of growth and development and of lessons learned.

Eschatological hope

The term *eschatological* refers to the end times, the final destiny of the soul and of humankind.[16] From this end-time perspective, evil and suffering are limited to human history. Ultimately, God has promised to bring an end to all suffering by destroying evil once and for all. At the end of time, God will make everything right. Essentially, this response means that our suffering is part of being human on this side of eternity. We can resist evil and suffering as a means of bringing God's future into our present. We can also endure and look to the future when "God shall wipe away all tears from their eyes; and there shall be no more death, neither sorrow, nor crying, neither shall there be any more pain: for the former things are passed away" (Revelation 2:4).

Limits of human understanding and affirmation of mystery

In this view, there is no serious attempt to address the difficulty inherent in theodicy. Those who ascribe to it admit their finite knowledge and understanding of God and the universe. They acknowledge that God's ways are not our ways and they are able to trust God, ultimately conceding to mystery. Such a stance allows hurting persons to affirm their pain, to grant God the right to be greater than human understanding, and to surrender to divine mystery.

OTHER RELIGIOUS OR
SPIRITUAL EXPLANATIONS

Randomness

Rabbi Harold Kushner, in his classic book, *When Bad Things Happen to Good People*,[17] offers the notion that some things happen for no reason and there is randomness in the universe. He writes, "Why must everything happen for a specific reason? Why can't we let the universe have a few rough edges?" Kushner did not blame God for the evil and suffering in the world. He made allowances for a God who may not yet be finished with creation, or who left a few "pockets of chaos" at the end of the 6th day of creation. For people who like to have things tied up in neat packages, Kushner's view creates the anxiety of not knowing. At the same time, it can be somewhat comforting to think that bad things happen randomly.

The will of God

Related to the problem of theodicy mentioned above is the notion of God's will. Many grievers make sense of their loss by claiming it is God's will. For some, this attribution is sufficient to provide a modicum of comfort. For others, it elicits irate fist-shaking at a deity who would somehow *will* the death of their child. The entire concept of the will of God has a tricky logic. If we say our children's deaths are the will of God, would we have said it was the will of God if they had been revived from the overdose and had not died? In my view, we cannot have it both ways. We have to get clear about how we understand this notion of the "will of God" because it reveals to us our beliefs about God's character and action.

I believe God's *intentional* will is for wholeness, health, love, peace, justice, community, respect, and abundant life for all of creation. In Luke 12:32 of the Christian testament we read, "Fear not, little flock; for it is your Father's good pleasure to give you the kingdom." God wants only good things for us and for all beings in the universe. God does not will illness, or war, or unjust systems of oppression, or addiction, or death. When contemplating that the idea that our child's death at the hands of heroin was God's will, we must ask ourselves, "What kind of God would intentionally dispense misery, frustration, illness, bereavement, or trauma on beloved children and then expect their parents to consider these tragedies God's will?" I do not believe in a God who *wills* our hearts to be broken. I believe in a God who permits suffering by creating us with autonomy and free will. I do not believe in a God who intervenes in the actions of billions of people, not to mention the atoms, cells, electrons, stars, and galaxies in a predetermined, scripted way. It is not that a sovereign Being *could not* exert this much control, but why? Why would God create us with the illusion of freedom, all the while controlling us like some divine puppeteer? Long ago I rejected this understanding of God, because as Leslie Weatherhead put it, "There is never any final comfort in a lie."[18]

"God needed him more" and other painful clichés

Sometimes well-meaning people try to help us answer the question, "Why did this happen?" by offering unhelpful, sometimes painful clichés that speak more to their discomfort with our grief than to any well-thought-out theology. I have been told in a pseudo-comforting way, "God needed another angel." Other well-intentioned acquaintances admonished me not to feel so bad because God needed Cameron more than I did. The latter statement made my blood boil. First, I was angry because, in a backhanded way, the person was denying my grief and pain—a normal and legitimate reaction to the death of my son. Second, the person was implying God's needs were somehow superior to my own and intimating I should graciously release my son into the hands of a needy God. I suspect she was also hinting at some divine reason for Cameron's death known only to God. Needless to say, these statements did more harm than good because they invalidated my experience and intensified my grief.

Other would-be comfort bearers told me Cameron was "in a better place" or "finally at peace." Again, I know these people had my best interest at heart. They did not intend to add to my pain. Nevertheless, they had no idea how these statements affected me. First, it made me even sadder to think *this place* was not good enough for him, *I* wasn't good enough for him, a future in this life was not good enough for him. I found myself asking, "If this life was not good enough, why did he enter it in the first place?" Second, I was disgusted by the presumptuousness of this statement. I had to bite my tongue so I would not blurt out, "How do *you know* he is in a better place? What if he is in a worse place?" That is no comforting thought to a mother who watched heroin hijack her son. Likewise, I wanted to believe Cameron was "finally at peace," and I hope that is the case. But I do not know for sure.

In my effort to make sense of Cameron's death, I have come to believe a confluence of factors led him to use, abuse, and fatally overdose on heroin. His death was the result of the elements described above: genetics, biology, chemistry, psychology, environment, choices, and behaviors. All these factors existed simultaneously within a larger context of interlocking cultural events that created what turned out to be the deadliest epidemic in U.S. history to date. Cameron's tragic, untimely death was not God's will. The God in whom I trust intended for Cameron to live a full, healthy, joyous, abundant life. And that God did not suspend the laws of nature to make an exception for my son. Instead, God gave him free will, which, in his case, had deleterious consequences.

I cannot hope to know the mind of the Divine short of my trust in pure goodness, love, light, justice, and peace. I am content not to have all of the answers and can accept the limits of human knowledge and affirm Divine mystery. In the final analysis, I have learned that the question, "Why did this happen?" is necessary but not sufficient for making meaning from loss. A more adequate question is, "Now that this tragedy has happened, how shall I respond to it?"

How Shall I Respond
to This Crisis?

Choosing our Attitudes

We have suffered enormous grief because of our children's deaths. We struggle to make sense of the loss as part of our healing journey. In the process, we confront the truth that suffering is inevitable and part of what it means to be human. Again and again we discover life's imperfections and unfairness. A significant step toward making meaning is in coming to tolerate the suffering and making room for the pain. In the midst of these difficult challenges, we discover a key to meaning-making: choosing our attitude toward our loss.

Victor Frankl, Holocaust survivor and author of *Man's Search for Meaning*,[19] believed we are free to choose the meaning we give to life's situations—even the tragic ones. He wrote, "Everything can be taken from man [sic] but one thing: the last of human freedoms—the ability to choose one's attitude in any given set of circumstances." When our loss leaves us feeling out of control, the fact that we can control our thoughts and our attitudes offers us a foothold on the arduous climb out of the pit of despair.

Frankl's philosophy is similar to the "perception" aspect of Patterson's Family Adjustment and Adaptation and Response (FAAR) model of resiliency described in chapter 5. There we learned that the story we tell ourselves about the crisis shapes our level of adaptation to it. I could tell the story about Cameron's life and death in a way that would result in self-blame and depression, keeping me from moving forward in any positive way. For example, my narrative about Cameron's death could feature a cruel and vengeful God who took my son as a punishment for his drug use. It could be a story about my failure as a parent who, as a mental health professional, *should have known* her son was an addict, but was not astute enough to get him help before it was too late. It could be a tale about a young man who did not have enough fortitude to stand up to his peers when they offered him drugs, and who, though he went to rehab and knew the deadly risk of heroin use, was not committed enough to his recovery to save his own life.

But that is not the way I *choose* to tell Cameron's story, our story. Instead, I can reframe the story as one that features parents who *chose* to adopt an infant who needed to be raised in a caring, stable home. It is a story about a boy who, as a child, was happy, inquisitive, engaging, funny, and often wise. It is a story about a child who, despite being surrounded by prodigious love, never felt worthy of that love. It is the story of an adolescent frustrated by academic struggles that contributed to poor self-esteem. It is an account of a youth well-loved by his friends and loyal beyond belief. It is a tale of a teen susceptible to peer influence, surrounded by easy access to substances, who self-medicated with pain pills and who could purchase heroin as easily as ordering a pizza. It is an epic story of love and loss and of how out of the ashes of anguish and heartbreak the phoenix of new life could arise. It is the story of learning to make room for ongoing pain and sadness and to frame them as evidence of love never lost. It is the narrative of embracing the mystery of the Divine, focusing less on believing beliefs and more on learning to trust. Mine is the story of redefining faith in the aftermath of death. No longer do I equate "faith" with absolute certainty or with holding fast to certain beliefs. Instead, on the other side of Cameron's death I agree with Mary Jean Irion that "faith is NOT *being sure*. It is _not being sure_, but betting with [my] last cent..."[20] The story is an emerging narrative of both discovering and creating a new "normal," and affirming the goodness of life, even in the stronghold of death. By choosing *this* story, I am able to say with the theologian and diplomat Dag Hammarskjold, "For all that has been, Thank you. For all that is to come, Yes!"

Benefit-finding

As stated earlier, Robert Neimeyer's benefit-finding refers to the ways we become able see positive outcomes in the aftermath of a crisis. Because the trajectory of each person's grief process is different, it is impossible to predict when one will be able to claim some positive benefit from the loss experience. This dimension of making meaning enables us to find the roses among the thorns, the diamonds among the stones.

Lichetenthal and Neimeyer, well-known grief experts, encouraged grievers to write in a journal about the benefit they had derived post-loss. They prompted writers to consider gifts that had emerged after loss, how their priorities had shifted, what qualities of resilience they had observed in themselves, how they had been supported by others, what lessons the deceased had taught them, and how the experience of loss had affected their sense of gratitude.[21]

In considering the prompts above, I decided to write my answers to these questions that could assist me in the benefit-finding dimension of making meaning of my loss. Here are my responses:

One of the unsought gifts that has come to me in the aftermath of Cameron's death is the knowledge that I am stronger and more courageous than I ever dared to dream. Before Cameron's death, I would have been certain I could not have survived losing him, even though it was my worst fear. Another gift has been learning who can tolerate my pain and whom I can count on to show up for me. A tragedy like the death of a child reveals the real selves of those around us. There have been a few surprises here. Some people, whom I expected to be present, have essentially abandoned me. Other people, with whom I had surface relationships, showed deep empathy and on-going compassion.

This experience of loss has shifted my priorities so I understand more clearly than ever before the notion that we are given only one day at a time. I know with my entire being how life can change in a literal heartbeat. This knowledge has made me more judicious about how I spend my time and with whom. It has also made me acutely aware of how important it is to tell people I love and care for them, and to express gratitude often and in as many ways possible. This loss has increased my awareness of my mortality and propelled me to "seize the day."

The qualities in myself that have contributed to my resilience have been my good health, my fairly moderate stressors, my commitment to self-care, my prior knowledge about grief and loss, my 40+ years of theological study and reflection, my ability to ask for help, and my determination to survive a parent's worst nightmare. Moreover, my belief in the ultimate triumph of good over evil and my trust that all will be well have enabled me to avoid blaming God for what happened to Cameron.

Others' supportive qualities have been their ways of checking in with me to inquire about how I am doing emotionally, remembering Cameron's death anniversary or his birthday, and acknowledging how sad I am on Mother's Day and every holiday without him. Another way others have supported me is through their witness to my parenting for over 20 years. During these years, they listened to my frustrations and doubts, my anguish about Cameron's struggles, and my fear for his safety. They have been bold enough to say to me, "I saw what you did for him, how much you loved him. You did everything you could. You were a *good* parent." These statements are not mere platitudes. They come from years of involvement and personal observation. Their words are a gracious antidote to my self-doubt.

One of the lessons Cameron taught me is that no love is

ever wasted or lost. His death taught me the cost of loving is high and worth it. I have learned just how precious life truly is. This tragedy has taught me that loss is inevitable and that the fear of loss is not reason enough to run away from relationships.

This loss has deepened my gratitude for the opportunity to be Cameron's mom and for all of the good memories we shared. I am grateful his addiction was only a fraction of who he was. I am grateful for those who are my closest friends and confidants, who dare to be genuine and vulnerable and invite me to do the same. It is to them I offer heartfelt appreciation. I am grateful for the beauty of the creation and for the opportunities I have to spend time outside in the natural world. I am grateful for all the places I find community and signs of grace. I am grateful for each new day of living.

By actually *writing* these responses, I gained clarity about the benefits that have come to me on this grief journey. Though I would give *anything* not to be traveling along this way, I am grateful that I am able to share my experiences through this book, with the hope that it may offer insights and support and companionship to others along the way.

QUESTIONS FOR REFLECTION:

» How have you made meaning of the loss of your child?

» How have you answered the question, "Why did this tragic death occur?"

» How have your religious or spiritual beliefs been a source of comfort for you?

» If religion or spirituality is not important to you, what beliefs or life philosophy has brought you comfort?

» To what degree have you wrestled with the problem of theodicy in the wake of the death of your child?

» What are your attitudes toward the tragedy that befell you and your family?

» How do you tell the story of your child's life and death?

» What positive outcomes have you discovered in the wake of grief?

CHAPTER 8:
REMEMBERING BY
DOING

COMING TO TERMS with our child's tragic death involves developing a narrative of what happened to our child and finding some meaning in this terrible loss. To learn to live successfully with the loss requires being able to acknowledge ways we have grown and changed and to articulate the positive outcomes that have come to us in the aftermath of our child's death. Although making sense of loss and finding positive outcomes can be emotionally challenging, research suggests those who do so fare better in the long run than those who do not. As part of this grief journey, there are many activities of remembrance by which we can keep our child's memory alive and continue our healing process.

Confronting Stigma

One of the most isolating aspects of losing a child to a drug overdose is the stigma associated with drug use, especially heroin. Because many people assume drug users are homeless derelicts inhabiting crime-ridden neighborhoods who are morally flawed, there is significant shame associated with drug addiction. Often we feel too embarrassed to share our pain, struggles, and loss because we worry about being misunderstood or rejected. We are aware some people may assume that those who die of an addiction are not as worthy of mourning as those who die from other causes. As stated earlier, we fear others consider us to be bad parents of bad kids. The truth is the opiate epidemic is running rampant in White, middle, and upper-middle-class suburban neighborhoods, in medium-sized cities, and in rural communities all over the United States.[1] Therefore, it is highly likely that our friends, acquaintances, and neighbors have some experience with drug addiction either in their families of origin or most certainly in their extended families. It is probable that everyone knows *someone* who struggles with an addiction.

Even though we may have intimate knowledge of what happens to people who become addicted to opiates, this knowledge does not make us immune to the stigma related to addiction. Such stigma is deeply entrenched in U. S. culture, so even those of us who know the truth about addiction are still vulnerable to holding the stigmatizing attitudes we have absorbed from our culture.

One of the most powerful ways of responding to our loss is to confront the stigma and to break the silence. Being courageous enough to tell others honestly what happened to our children releases us from the feeling of "being the only one" who has undergone the frustration, the helplessness, the agony, the expense, the fear, and the despair of loving a child with an unrelenting addiction to heroin or other drugs. When we dare to speak openly about our child, what we endured, and especially of our untimely, devastating loss, we invite others to share their stories. As a result, we discover others who truly understand our experiences because they, too, have experienced a similar loss. Moreover, we discover community among others who suffered similar losses and find strength to speak the truth. This truth-telling is the first step toward breaking the silence that keeps us isolated and changing perceptions about who uses drugs and what addiction does to individuals, families, and communities.

Learning About Addiction

Given what most of us have been through with our child's addiction, we may assume we know all there is to know about addiction. We certainly have had firsthand experience of the ways heroin and other drugs hijack our children's brains and turn them into strangers who become desperate for drugs to survive. We know about the pills, the petty crimes, the dope-sick days, the jail time, the failed rehab, the good intentions, the deception, and the relapses. We also need to learn more about the physiology of addiction and just what happens to the brain on drugs. Being armed with information about the chemical processes in the brain that create addiction, we can assist in reducing stigma by correcting others' misconceptions about substance use disorders. Also, we become more prepared to talk honestly with others and enable them to understand our powerlessness over our child's addiction. Being able to accept the difficult truth that all the money and love in the world cannot always triumph over addiction may help us forgive ourselves and chip away at the stigma surrounding death by overdose.

Being Assertive

Another way to confront the stigma of our child's substance use problem is to be assertive in the face of unhelpful comments. When well-meaning friends, family members, and acquaintances make statements intended to be supportive but instead have the effect of being hurtful, often we brush them off rather than challenging them. For example, I bristle when someone tells me "everything (including Cameron's death from a heroin overdose) happens for a reason." If I were to speak honestly about my reaction to this remark, I would ask, "What kind of reason for my son's death would bring me comfort?" So many of the "reasons" offered increased my pain rather than made me feel supported. Maybe there is some unknowable, cosmic, or metaphysical reason hidden in the mind of the Divine, or maybe there is no reason at all. Regardless, being told Cameron's death "happened for a reason" only makes me annoyed. It does not offer me any solace. In order to be more assertive, I will need to respond to the "everything-happens-for-a-reason" comment by asking, "Could you give me an example of a *reason*?" Or perhaps I would just tell the speaker I don't share that belief and that it makes me feel unsupported. Whatever unhelpful comments make us feel uncomfortable or make us feel our pain is being dismissed, we can confront. We do not have to swallow our hurt. Instead, we have the opportunity to help well-intended people learn what is and is not appropriate when relating to mourners.

Becoming An Activist

An activist is someone who holds strong beliefs about an issue and engages in activities to promote social or political change. While it may not mean taking to the streets with a hand-painted sign, there are ways we can take action. We can become involved in efforts to effect change in the way opiates are prescribed. We can report abuses in sober homes such as unethical marketing or when clients are put on the street for relapsing. We can seek change in legislation that makes substance-use problems criminal and results in little to no treatment. All of these are ways we can harness our grief for a positive purpose. We can get involved in local initiatives in our own cities where others are becoming instrumental in increasing awareness of the opiate problem and are attempting to do something about it. We can become engaged in efforts to educate community members about substance-use disorders and assist them in understanding that these problems are not the result of moral failure or a lack of willpower but a very real disease affecting the brain. We can connect with other grieving parents to form anti-drug coalitions for change in local and state communities. The website NOPE (Narcotics Overdose Prevention and Education, http://www.nopetaskforce.org/) is an example of such involvement. We may develop websites for information, support, political action, or resources to both build community and offer others solidarity in their struggles. Taking concrete action is both a way of assisting others and finding a positive outlet for our grief.

Engaging in Rituals

A ritual is a symbolic act that creates an emotional connection between people to serve a purpose such as facilitating grief expression. Rituals are powerful because through their action they are able to capture beliefs and feelings that cannot be expressed in words. Rituals surrounding grief are numerous and imbedded in cultural and religious practices. Usually one considers the funeral or memorial service to be the religious ritual of choice immediately following a death. However, ongoing rituals as one traverses the grief path also aid mourners in coping with loss.

There are many ways rituals can be used during the grief process. Creating rituals that help us stay connected with our deceased children and may be important as we remember our children's birthdays or the anniversaries of their deaths. These private ritual activities may include lighting a candle or participating in a guided meditation.

Simple rituals have been important to me in remembering Cameron. Because he loved nature, I plan an activity that will get me outdoors on the anniversary of his death. On the first anniversary of his death, I took a challenging day hike in the mountains of Colorado. Standing on top of that peak with a magnificent 360-degree perspective made me feel connected with his spirit in a place he loved.

Another ritual I engage in on Cameron's birthday is to eat his favorite foods. Sometimes I prepare eggs Benedict for breakfast. Other times, I eat in an Indian restaurant. When I visit the site where we scattered his ashes, often I take along a packet of the herb rosemary to scatter as a symbol of remembrance.

As we plod through our grief experience, we may create rituals to help us move forward. When faced with several boxes of children's books Cameron had loved, I agonized over what to do with them. I hung on to them for many, many months, thumbing through them from time to time and being overcome with the memories they evoked. I had always thought I would save these marvelous books for future grandchildren. However, Cameron's death ended that possibility. Finally, in a symbolic act of remembrance and release, I decided to send the books to Cameron's former girlfriend who had just given birth to a son. When I was finally ready, it was with a sense of joy that I was able to part with those books, knowing that another boy would love them and Cameron's legacy would continue.

Rituals of letting go can also be powerful acts of healing. We can let go of our anger and disappointment that our children did not grow and flourish as we had hoped and planned. We can let go of the ways we were hurt by their behavior while they were using substances. We can design this ritual to be done in private or shared with friends and family members.

Another variation on this ritual is to engage in a Watch Night worship experience, which is held in many churches on New Year's Eve. The purpose of these services is for individuals to review the year that has passed and make confessions, ask forgiveness, and greet the New Year with prayer and a commitment to renewal. Although designed in different ways, often there are opportunities to write on slips of paper things in our lives we would like to release. Then, at the close of the worship experience, the slips of paper are burned, symbolizing forgiveness and mercy. This particular ritual can be emotionally intense, so it is advisable to plan to have supportive people nearby to help process the experience.

Rituals can be developed for any purpose in the grief process. They can be public or private. We can use music or dance or art or poetry or fire. We can gather in a garden, a meadow, a mountaintop, the seashore, a park, a home, a place of worship, or any location that holds a positive association for us. We can design any kind of ritual that helps us honor our deceased child and keep alive the memories.

Creating Memory Collections

Concrete memories of our deceased children bring us both joy and sadness in remembering. One way to keep alive the connection to our children is to do something intentional that invites us to gather cherished memories in one place. We can accomplish this goal in many ways: through memory boxes, scrapbooks, photo books and calendars, music, and quilts.

Memory Boxes

Jordan Potash and Stephanie Handel describe the creation of decorated memory boxes into which we put mementos of our deceased child.[2] The box can be any size or shape and made from any materials such as a wooden box or a craft box. Individuals decorate the boxes using colors, materials, words, or symbols that are reminiscent of the loved one. Inside the box, we place items that were special to our children or remind us of them: pictures, their drawings, sporting mementos, letters, greeting cards, or any other tangible items that hold special meaning. The box may be public or private, and we may consider creating a ritual of opening it on special days such as anniversaries, birthdays, and holidays.

An Anthology of Stories

We can create a loose-leaf memory book or purchase a journal to record memories and stories about the life of our child. We can decorate it elaborately or keep it simple. Here, not only do we write our own memories, but we invite others to share in creating the anthology. We can record the memories of family members, teachers, coaches, Scout leaders, and friends by asking them to share a story with us about our child. The memories shared can be inspiring, humorous, frightening, or endearing. As we move through the grief process, we discover there was much about our child we did not know. There are stories of generosity, love, loyalty, and friendship. There are tales of adolescent capers and childhood exploration. What we discover as we move through the grief process is how important it is to continue remembering and to keep the connection with our child's memory vital.

Photo Books or Collages

Another memory-collection activity is making a photo book or collage. This activity requires reviewing photos of the deceased across their lifespan and selecting special photos that capture our loved one. The photos designated for the book or display may include life highlights such as birthday parties, family travel, sports, recitals, Scouting activities, holidays, graduations, weddings, and other special moments. The photos may be organized chronologically or by theme. If choosing a photo book, many online companies sell these products and provide technical assistance with the tasks of uploading photos, choosing a background and layout, inserting textboxes, and adding embellishments. A photo display may be created as a large single-frame collage or a multiple-frame gallery featuring selected photos. Regardless of the method chosen, each project invites us to view our child's life in photos and to produce a photo-based keepsake.

A little over two years after Cameron's death, I was involved in an accident that resulted in a fractured ankle. After the first medical examination, I knew I would be immobilized for a few months and confined to a small bedroom on the lower level of our home. That is when I realized I would be forced to slow down long enough to work on a photo book of Cameron's life. The task was immense. There were many boxes of photo albums I had carefully maintained for 26 years. And I had a few shoeboxes of recent random photos that never made it into albums. Reviewing the photos was bittersweet. The process took me back through so many wonderful memories of Cameron as a baby, a toddler, a young child, a preteen, an adolescent, a young man. There were many fun events and exciting family travel experiences. By immersing myself in this family history, I was able to celebrate Cameron's *whole* life and not be focused totally on the downward spiral of his addiction to heroin. I was able to see the delightful, loving, caring boy, and remember his infectious laugh. It took many hours over several weeks to complete the photo book, and it has become one of my most treasured belongings. I have been able to share it with friends and family, some who knew Cameron and some who did not. Moreover, I have the book on the coffee table where it is always within my reach. Now Cameron's smiling face looks out at me each time I sit on the sofa. All of these images have come alive rather than continued to be buried at the bottom of boxes in a storage unit.

Memory Quilts

The memory quilt, constructed from the deceased child's clothing, typically tee shirts, is another project for the memory collection. Those who have the time, interest, and skill to make the quilt are doubly blessed. For those who do not, there are many online companies as well as local quilters who can fashion the fabrics into a wonderful collage of memories. Essentially, the memory quilt involves sorting through the child's clothing and selecting favorite garments, logos, or designs that represent the deceased. Usually the quilter requests the entire garment to be sent unaltered. That way, the quilter can cut appropriately sized squares, apply the required backing, and organize them into a unique design. This project can be somewhat expensive if one must pay a quilter to create it. However, it is a way of being surrounded by happy memories. And, like the photo book, it offers us a glimpse of the good times and reminds us of special moments and experiences. It also becomes a wonderful thing to wrap up in on days we need comfort.

When Cameron was a young child, long before the notion of drug use ever crossed my mind, I began saving Cameron's favorite tee shirts with the plan to have them made into a quilt for his high school graduation present. Boxes of tee shirts accumulated over the years. Finally, as he began his senior year in high school, I sought out a quilter who could create my long-planned tee shirt quilt. I shipped Cameron's favorite shirts and those representative of his school, camp, sports teams, and travel off to the quilter in another state. Several weeks later, my cherished dream quilt arrived. On graduation day, when I presented it to Cameron, he was delighted. The years passed, and as he began to slip into substance use, one day he returned the quilt and asked me to "keep it for him." I have had it ever since that day. Despite this quilt being crafted prior to Cameron's death, I am so grateful to have it now. Those who struggle with discarding a deceased child's clothing may want to consider a memory quilt.

After Cameron's death, I was sorting through what was left of his clothing and came across stacks of boxer shorts of various colors and designs. For years, I had a tradition of sending him holiday boxers, his favorite sports team boxers, or souvenir boxers from my travels. Thus, in addition to the tartan plaids, there were Halloween boxers with skeletons, Christmas boxers with holly, and boxers with a map of the Paris subway! Soon I came up with the idea of a variation on the memory quilt. I decided to ask a friend who is an accomplished seamstress to make a set of travel pillows using a patchwork pattern made from an assortment of Cameron's boxer shorts. The result was a wonderful pillow to clip on to my carry-on bag. Every time I travel with it, someone notices and asks about it. Then I can tell the story again, thus cementing the ongoing bond with my son. These memory collections may be helpful to younger siblings or children of the deceased so that they may have tangible reminders of the loved one they lost.

Music Playlists

Music is an especially evocative medium, capable of eliciting a variety of emotions. It can be a means of both reminding us of our loss and drawing us into a life beyond loss. Joy Berger[3] suggested putting together a group of songs, or playlist, reminiscent of the deceased loved one. The songs can be saved on smartphones, iTunes, and other music applications and played at will. The songs we select can be drawn from any music genre. They may be our loved one's favorite songs or songs that remind us of our child, or our loss. In addition, the playlist may contain uplifting music that speaks to us of endurance, hope, faith, triumph, and new life beyond our devastating loss. We may already know song titles we want to include. Or, we may need to search online or ask friends and family for suggestions. The important aspect of this activity is to look for songs that have the potential to capture and express our deepest emotions. The music may be played as part of ritual remembrances on anniversaries, birthdays, or other special days, or it may be played when one is overwhelmed by the sadness of grief, or when one seeks comfort or to be inspired to continue the journey of transformation.

Gathering Social Media Support

Certainly, social media has transformed the way people of all ages communicate with each other and share their lives. At times, social media such as Facebook, Twitter, and Instagram can be fun: They connect us to family, friends, co-workers, and acquaintances who have touched our lives and help us know what is transpiring in their lives. We learn about the birth of children and grandchildren, see photos of exotic travel destinations, share celebrations like birthdays, holidays, and weddings, and the antics of well-loved pets. Other times, social media can be annoying as we scroll through screen after screen of political posts, advertisements for products or services, or sensationalized stories about people we don't know. Sometimes social media posts are just plain trivial. I do not need to know what my friends ate for dinner. However, in the years since Cameron's death, I have found social media to be a comfort on the tender days such as the anniversary of his death or his birthday. I find I can post something about missing him and ask those who knew him to share a memory. The responses are uplifting, help keep the connections strong, and create a community of shared remembrance despite the distance between those who knew and loved him.

Writing Opportunities

In general, grieving individuals who write about their loss experience improved mental and physical health. Two kinds of writing offer avenues for exploring grief reactions as well as providing healing moments and new understandings and meanings derived from the grief experience.

Journaling

Journaling allows one to select the content and approach of written reflections about loss. It offers the opportunity to sort through conflicting emotions, release tension, get in touch with memories, create a lasting record of one's grief journey, and develop deeper self-understanding. Because a journal is intended to be private, it provides a safe place to process one's inner thoughts without censure. Writing about grief helps us to tell our own story and to understand our own thoughts and feelings. We can include poetry, quotations, musical lyrics, drawings, illustrations, photographs, or anything that comes to mind when we approach the journaling activity. Rereading our journal entries provides evidence of how far we've come in wrestling with our grief.

Blogging
A blog is a regularly updated online journal or diary shared with the world. It can be anything one wants it to be; however, for those grieving, most often it is a medium through which to share one's grief journey with others. Blogging affords regular people the opportunity for a global audience to receive an account of their thoughts, feelings, and experiences.

Starting a blog is fairly simple and there are many sites offering assistance with set up.[4] Essentially, blogging requires first selecting a domain name easily recognized by the public (usually ones ending in .com, .net or .org) and then deciding on a web host where the blog will "live" online. Some web-hosting offers are free and others require a nominal monthly fee. For those unfamiliar with blogging, it is helpful to consult with someone knowledgeable in the field or to use an online guide. After establishing the basic blog setup, one decides on themes and appearance attractive to the target audience. Some people design a logo associated with their blog so readers are drawn to the blog's personal "branding."

The beauty of blogging is the freedom to be expressive without having to be perfect. It is a mechanism for connecting with people the world over drawn to a common interest or theme. Blogging is a means of releasing thoughts and feelings without judgment. Bloggers can share their grief experiences and connect with others undergoing similar losses. Some people use blogs as they would use journals, except journals are usually private and blogs are public, though some bloggers choose to use a pseudonym rather than reveal their true identities. Regardless of the format used, writing is a powerful means of managing grief.

Engaging in Expressive Arts

Some grievers find welcomed release by engaging in artistic activities. Getting involved in yoga or a form of dance involves the entire body in movement toward healing. The well-known connection between body, mind, and spirit comes together when we are using our bodies artistically to express ourselves. Other arts, such as drawing, painting, sculpting, or building provide outlets for self-expression.

All the various activities described in this chapter serve to cement our connection with our deceased child and to harness the energy of our grief into action. These activities help us be intentional about ways we remember and celebrate our child's life, share our grief, and honor the transformed persons we are becoming.

Questions for Reflection:

» In what ways have you identified your internalized stigma about your child's substance use and addiction?

» How have you attempted to address the stigma with others?

» What steps have you taken or do you plan to take to become more knowledgeable about drugs and addiction?

» How have you been or can you be assertive when someone makes a well-meaning statement you find painful or offensive?

» What rituals, private or public, have you engaged in as you remember your child? What new rituals might you create?

» What memory collections have you created? What kinds seem appealing to you? Why?

» If you use social media (Facebook, Instagram, LinkedIn, Snapchat), how have you found it to be a source of support for you on the tender days of remembrance?

» What types of writing have you used to process your grief?

» Consider responding to these questions in your journal:

- What do you remember telling yourself about your child's death when you first learned about it? What are you telling yourself now?

- What religious or spiritual beliefs have shaped the way you make meaning of your child's death? What, if anything, has changed over time as you process this loss?

- How has the loss of your child been a catalyst for your personal growth?

- What kind of changes have you undergone as you have weathered this season of grief?

CHAPTER 9:
LIFE AFTER LOSS: PATHWAYS TO ADAPTATION, GROWTH AND THE "NEW NORMAL"

THE DEATH OF one's child unwittingly creates a dividing line between life "before" loss and life "after" loss. The seismic effect[1] of this tumultuous loss, along with the lifelong "aftershocks," shakes the foundations of all surviving parents' lives. The beliefs, assumptions, worldviews, hopes, dreams, and plans we held before are forever shattered, and the ground beneath our feet feels unstable and unpredictable. We are flung into this new territory, forced to regain our footing on the shifting sands. Eventually the shaking of the foundations stops. The rumbling and thunderous cacophony quiets, and we begin picking up the pieces of our fractured lives and start the agonizing process of rebuilding.

The goal of our journey in the aftermath of this unparalleled upheaval is to live into a new form of well-being. This well-being is characterized by less anxiety and depression and debilitating sadness. It is also marked by improved overall physical health. Reestablishing well-being for grievers involves reengaging in meaningful relationships, getting involved in life-affirming activities, keeping our bond with our deceased child, and experiencing personal growth as one integrates the loss into a "new normal." Determining the level of one's well-being after loss is somewhat subjective. However, comparing one's post-loss functioning and relationships with those pre-loss can help us gauge how we are doing.

One of the signs of integration is our ability to manage our routines to function competently as parents, spouses, co-workers, colleagues and friends. Another clue about our adaptation to loss is how well we are able to accomplish the tasks of daily living. A further key to improved well-being is to have regained some degree of meaning, enjoyment, and fulfillment in our lives.

Another hint about our adaptation to loss is if we are able to look back on the terrible tragedy that befell us and detect ways in which we have experienced positive growth or change. The presence of growth and positive outcomes does not nullify pain, sadness, and distress. These dimensions of grief remain. However, many of us living with loss can point to transformation that has occurred as we have traversed the highways and byways of grief.

Themes of Positive Change

At some time after the death of their child, many bereaved parents come to the realization they can see that some phoenixes of good have emerged from the ashes of loss. These positive outcomes may have occurred in us as individuals, in our relationships, emotional life, spirituality and life philosophy.

Individual Changes

Although those who have suffered a significant loss may be more emotionally vulnerable during subsequent losses, many grievers reported seeing themselves as stronger and possessing more coping ability than they ever believed they had. Just the fact that they survived their worst nightmare often gives grievers a sense of agency and resilience. Some grievers have said they experienced a greater appreciation for the fragility of life and a sharp awareness that death is always a heartbeat away. If before Cameron's death I had been asked how I thought I would manage that potential tragedy, I would have thought I could not survive it. However, as the mother of a son addicted to heroin, the thought of his possible death by overdose had crossed my mind numerous times. Usually, I dismissed the notion of Cameron's potential death with a prayer that he would get into an effective rehab and commit to getting clean and sober. When the horrific call came informing me that my nightmare had come true, I was devastated, and I knew in that moment my life was forever changed.

Over the months and years that have followed, I was amazed at my resilience. I knew I possessed many of the personal qualities associated with the ability to adapt to crisis; however, I was not convinced of my personal fortitude until day by day I got up each morning and responded to the day's demands. Looking back, I now see how my self-confidence has grown. I believe I have become acutely aware of how precious life is and how everything can change suddenly and without warning. Thus, I have become intentional in doing things I want to do, seeing people I want to see, and visiting places I want to visit. *Carpe Diem* has become more than a motto. It has become a way of life. Because I have been forced to face such a significant loss, I find myself less afraid of death and more able to view it as an inevitable part of life.

Relationship Changes

People who have experienced devastating losses have a heightened awareness of relationships and often feel a stronger connection with family and friends in the aftermath of the crisis. In a sense, tragedies have the capacity to bring people together and encourage them to express their thoughts and feelings.

My experience managing my grief certainly reflects important social connections. The social support from those who care for me has been tremendous. I have felt so fortunate to have people in my life invite me to share my pain, and to talk about what life after loss is like. In the safety of those relationships, I have been empowered to be more self-disclosing and more compassionate toward others who are hurting.

Emotional Life

A potential positive outcome of grief is to learn about and experience a vast array of emotions. During grief, often we learn to let go of fear or embarrassment about expressing our feelings, and we come to understand how changeable our feelings are.

Because of my background, training, and experience as a counselor, I had a wealth of knowledge about emotions prior to Cameron's death. However, after experiencing such emotional trauma, I became more attuned to what a myriad of feelings *feels* like. Moreover, one of my most important discoveries was the ability to experience multiple, even conflicting feelings simultaneously. I learned I could feel sad on Cameron's birthday, as well as feel happy about going hiking or to the beach on that day to honor him. I could feel angry that his life was cut short by heroin, all the while feeling grateful to have had him as long as I did.

Spirituality and Life Philosophy

Grievers' spirituality, religion, and personal life philosophies have surfaced as significant factors in the grief journey. In one study of approximately 300 adults, 80% said religion and spiritual beliefs helped them during grief. Others claimed they had experienced a personal transformation with more deeply held values and beliefs.[2]

Having a theology degree and having served as a local church pastor for many years provided me with both knowledge and experience in the areas of religion, spirituality, and grief. I had struggled intellectually with the problem of suffering and had spent many hours in hospitals and homes holding the hands of the dying and their family members. When I found myself in a similar situation, I was relieved to find my long-held religious and spiritual beliefs and my trust in God were able to keep me afloat. When I shared the news of Cameron's death with family and friends, I remember distinctly writing, "I trust all will yet be well."

What I did not expect in the aftermath of Cameron's death was openness to new forms of spirituality, an interest in exploring different concepts of the afterlife, and a willingness to be led on new spiritual paths. In fact, one of the positive outcomes of my grief experience has been delving into the beliefs and practices of other religious and spiritual traditions and learning how my own spirituality can be deepened and enhanced.

On the day we learn of the death of our child, "normal" life ends. There is no way we can possibly believe anything positive will ever emerge from the pit of desolation, pain, devastation, and despair. Yet, as grievers navigate their loss, many discover unforeseen blessings and positive aftereffects.

What Others Have Done to Cope Effectively with Loss

In a study of 397 adults averaging 13 months post-loss, researchers asked them what they had done to help themselves manage their grief. Some people said they had tried to get back into some semblance of a routine by going to work or school. Some engaged in activities that kept their loved one's memory such as looking at pictures. Others reported they talked about their loved one, cried, and grieved. Some sought counseling or joined support groups. In essence, about half of the coping approaches to managing grief involved engaging in and trying to maintain some semblance of normalcy by continuing routines.[3] The researchers concluded that both embracing and turning away from the loss led to positive outcomes.

It was comforting to me to read findings from the above study about how people coped with loss. I had a very similar experience. First, as soon as possible after Cameron's death, I got back into my routine and got caught up on my work. The predictability of both routine and work created the stability I needed when the rest of my world felt unhinged. Second, I worked on my photo book chronicling Cameron's life—a project that took many hours over several months. This endeavor elicited both smiles and tears as I journeyed backward, reviewing a treasured life with him. Third, I began writing this book, which, because it focuses on grief, was both cathartic and healing. Fourth, I did my share of turning away from loss as I engaged in planning travel adventures, visiting friends, and shopping for a new home. Both the turning toward and turning away from grief helped me find the balance I needed to move along my life's path.

Forging a Healthy, Happy New Normal

Even though the death of our children tears open our hearts and shatters our lives, most of us discern ways of coping that work for us. We can look back at the trauma and see signs of positive growth, and eventually we carve out new ways of being in the world and living with the dreadful loss we experienced. As we move along our new path, we discover there are proven behaviors that result in greater happiness and improved health and longevity. Some of these insights are revealed in a book entitled *Why Good Things Happen to Good People* by Stephen Post and Jill Neimark.[4] Here the authors offer scientific support for the power of unselfish love and giving to enhance health and happiness. For example, they reported *giving* reduced mortality significantly in later life, even when the giving started late.

Post and Neimark discussed several ways of giving that have been shown to result in increased health, happiness, well-being and longevity. For me, gratitude, forgiveness, courage, humor, compassion and expressiveness have been the most transformative.

Gratitude

Gratitude is acknowledging all that has occurred that makes it possible to wake up and live another day. Gratitude is a sure way of balancing joy and sorrow. In fact, those who keep "gratitude journals" find themselves happier, more optimistic, sleep better, and feel more connected to others.[5]

Through the refiner's fire of loss, I have become intensely aware of how much there is for which to be thankful. Although I have not been as disciplined as the gratitude journal keepers, regularly I offer thanks for the blessings that have come to me: life, health, education, resources, friends, family, faith, and so many more.

"It is not happiness that makes us grateful.
It is gratefulness that makes us happy. "
- Brother David Steindl-Rast

At a church in my community, one of the worship leaders brought in a donut and showed it to the children who gathered there. She directed attention to the hole in the donut and commented on the fact that part of it was missing. Her point, of course, was to teach the children and to remind the adults that we can choose to be grateful for what we have (the donut) or focus on what is missing (the hole). In every way I can, I am *choosing* to make gratitude a priority because I have experienced its positive benefits.

"What's lost is nothing to what's found, and
all the death that ever was, set next to life,
would scarcely fill a cup."
- Fredrick Buechner
Godric, p. 96

Forgiveness

Forgiveness involves letting go of the harm we have suffered and moving from bitterness to joy. Surely, forgiveness is a process, not an instantaneous act. Forgiveness is not forgetting, condoning, excusing, or reconciling if it is not in our best interest. Forgiveness involves examining our hurt and acknowledging how we have been harmed. It includes deciding what forgiveness means to us—what it is and what it is not. It may require the effort of taking the perspective of the one who hurt us and attempting to understand that person's situation, motive, or stressors that contributed to our wounding. Seeing the offender as someone with whom we share common humanity may enable us to offer grace and mercy.

Those of us who have lost our children have been deeply hurt and wounded. We have looked for someone, anyone, to blame: our children, our spouses, God, our children's friends, drug dealers, law enforcement, rehab counselors, ourselves. The challenge of living into forgiveness has incredible benefits. According to Post and Neimark, the results of over 1400 scientific studies reveal that forgiving others improves health more than being forgiven. Forgiveness alleviates depression, boosts mood, and reduces anger. It lowers stress hormones and helps us maintain close relationships. Though forgiving others and ourselves is a difficult endeavor, the ultimate outcomes improve our overall well-being.

The process of forgiving myself for everything I could have done or not done to prevent Cameron's death has been challenging. As parents, it is so easy to blame ourselves when something terrible happens to our children. Even if the thoughts are illogical or impossible, they still haunt us. These "if onlys" and "what ifs" can stunt our growth, and they can keep us spiraling downward in the vortex of grief. Surely there were things we could have done differently, and hindsight provides great revelation. However, continuing to batter ourselves emotionally interferes with healing. Whenever one of these self-blaming thoughts arises, I acknowledge it and then dismiss it. I find I need to forgive myself for whatever ways I failed Cameron and be more gracious and merciful to myself when I am feeling caught in the quagmire of guilt.

Working on forgiving others is important, too. Every story of death by drug overdose involves a cast of actors playing various roles in the unfolding tragedy. In Cameron's story, there were the wardens who released him from jail inappropriately, putting him out on the street after months of being incarcerated and drug free. There were the drug-using peers who took him in and helped him procure the heroin. There was the young man using with him that fateful night who, when he discovered Cameron overdosing and struggling for life, abandoned him in an empty garage. And there was Cameron himself making fatal choices out of habit, or desperation, or both. I am working very hard to forgive all of those who contributed to Cameron's tragic death. I acknowledge the anger that seethes in me when I think that if only one of them had done something different, the outcome could have been different. It could have been different, but it wasn't. And, given Cameron's trajectory, the same outcome was likely, only with another story and other players.

Because I know and believe in the healing power of forgiveness, I am committed to the process regardless of how long it takes. For me, forgiveness is not instant absolution. It involves acknowledging pain-inflicted lives forever altered and a violation of trust. Essentially, forgiving others means we let go of the burden of ill will and negative feelings about others. We forgive because it enables us to be free. Offering forgiveness is a door out of the pit of despair, so I pursue it diligently.

> *"Until we can forgive the person who harmed us, that person will hold the keys to our happiness; that person will be our jailor."*[6]
> - Archbishop Desmond Tutu, *The Book of Joy*

Courage
Courage is born of inner strength, resilience, hardiness, and the ability to risk our emotional safety in order to endure the pain and the terrible circumstances of life. It is out of the crucible of crisis that we emerge stronger. It is by daring to get up each day and face its demands that we reveal our bravery.

Sometimes courage means rethinking our life's purpose and our personal mission, especially when we find ourselves on the other side of a significant loss. We may feel called to confront the sources of substance abuse in our communities, ask for support from our local, state and national leaders, or spearhead a movement to *do something* about the heroin epidemic that is destroying an entire generation.

Courage in the face of such incredible loss means taking on something bold and even terrifying in order to speak the truth. For me, embarking on writing this book and sharing the intimate details of the pain of loss and the path of resilience has been a courageous act. Making space in my life for whatever comes of it will also take courage. Courage doesn't mean not being fearful. It is *being* fearful and moving ahead anyway.

Humor

Humor is a way of connecting with joy. Humor is healing because it keeps us grounded in the present, it elevates the secretion of hormones that make us feel good, and it reduces the stress hormone cortisol. Humor and laughter are linked to better heart-health, higher self-esteem. and improved psychological well-being.[7] Giving ourselves permission to enjoy light-hearted moments and funny movies, cartoons, or sayings can lift our mood and connect us to others.

In one study on humor, Kaye Herth discovered light-heartedness was a necessary component in dealing successfully with difficult life events.[8] Incorporating humor into our lives is a means of managing disappointments, discouragement, and setbacks. It can become the powerful antidote to our prolonged sadness.

One of my best qualities is my sense of humor. I believe it is my father's legacy. He always seemed to manage tense moments with a burst of wry humor. Even when I feel wrapped in a blanket of sadness, I try never to miss an opportunity to see the humorous. I find that the lightheartedness humor provides is a wonderful means of escaping from the heaviness of grief. I have a cartoon collection I can go to when I need cheering. Also, I enjoy searching for humorous greeting cards for special friends—a hobby that affords laughter all year long. I have found that researchers are right about the power of humor to relieve stress.

Kindness

Practicing kindness has been one of the most positive outcomes for me from Cameron's death. Although I would have said I was generally a "kind" person prior to Cameron's death, I'm grateful to Joanne Cacciatore for the inspiration of her "Kindness Project"[9] that cemented the practice for me. Since 1996, the Kindness Project has been a way for grieving parents to honor their children who have died. There have been over one million participants in the project from various countries. Cacciatore designed a card to be given to a recipient of a random act of kindness done in memory of the deceased child. I created a variation on her card. Mine read, "This random act of kindness is offered in memory of Brian Cameron Frame, November 20, 1986-August 9, 2013. The reverse side of the card reads, "Pay It Forward." In addition to distributing the cards when I completed a random act of kindness like taking bagels to my car mechanic's garage, I sent two cards to some of my closest friends asking them to participate in honor of Cameron's birthday. Not only did I experience joy in the project myself, I was doubly blessed by the stories friends shared of their engagement in the Kindness

Project in Cameron's honor. Having been part of this project myself, I agree with Cacciatore that through the random acts of kindness the bereaved are able to experience love, compassion, and hope.

Compassion

Compassion is our empathic, caring response to others' pain or distress. Brain imaging studies reveal that we are hardwired for compassion. Compassion calms us and connects us emotionally in our bonding and nurturing relationships. Compassion makes it possible to mirror or reflect others' emotions. It increases our own positive emotions, moves us to behave kindly and generously, and is connected to spirituality.

"Compassion is a sense of concern that arises when we are confronted with another's suffering and feel motivated to see that suffering relieved."[10]
--Thupten Jinpa
A Fearless Heart: How the Courage to Be Compassionate Can Transform Our Lives

I have been challenged to cultivate compassion for those with substance use disorders, those like Cameron who struggle with opiate abuse. Theirs is a culture largely unfamiliar and frightening to me. My grief journey is requiring me to develop more and more empathy and understanding for those caught in the web of addiction. Although losing Cameron to this dreadful affliction could cause me to push heroin users away, I realize my challenge is to develop more reverence for them.

One of the byproducts of undergoing a significant loss such as the death of a child is a new level of compassion for others' suffering. When we learn of other parents' losses, we feel an immediate connection to their pain and may be led to reach out to them because we, too, have known pain. Cultivating compassion in ourselves by making intentional decisions to engage with the suffering of others creates new levels of bonding, interpersonal connection, and increased well-being.

His Holiness the Dalai Lama pointed out that when we focus exclusively on our own pain we increase our suffering. But, when we inquire about how we can help others, even when we are in anguish, the compassion transforms our pain.

Sharing others' suffering has deepened my compassion for those experiencing grief. While I am particularly drawn to grieving parents, I have become intentional about reaching out to those who have experienced the death of loved ones and other losses. On one of the anniversaries of Cameron's death, a friend sent me a small packet of rosemary, indicating that rosemary was for "remembrance." On the tiny envelope an inscription read, "Contents may be scattered at the gravesite or any place of shared remembrance. The act of scattering some and keeping the rest symbolically recognizes 'Love that will forever live…some to keep and some to give.'"[11] I was so touched by this small token of memory, I ordered a box of rosemary packets and began recording the anniversaries of friends' and family members' losses. Then I began sending the packets to them on their loved ones' death anniversaries. This small act of compassion has helped me to stand with others in their grief and to lessen my own.

Expressiveness

Imagination, playfulness, flexibility, and creativity lead us toward expressing ourselves in various ways. When we allow ourselves to be immersed in drawing, painting, music, dance, sculpting, or writing, we tap into places in our hearts that often aren't available to our heads. Expressing ourselves through creative outlets may reduce our anxiety, depression or stress.

Writing is perhaps the most creative outlet I've engaged in since Cameron's death. True to the research about it, writing provides a means of coming to terms with loss, expressing feelings, sharing experiences, and forging a new way of being in the world. Making the memory book of Cameron's life, too, provided a creative outlet. My hope is that by writing this book, others who have been struck by the tidal wave of grief may find in it life support to keep them afloat.

Being intentional about honing our skills in these many facets of giving almost guarantees an improvement in our overall well-being and opens a space for joy in lives rent apart by sorrow.

Conclusion

I began this book with the heart-rending story of my son's descent into the hell of heroin overdose and death. It is a story shared by thousands of other parents whose children have been lost to this demonic drug. Through our experiences as grieving parents, we are able to acknowledge the stigma associated with a death through drug overdose. We have confronted the guilt we feel for not having done more for our children. We have been embarrassed because of the relief that comes from knowing that our children are finally free from their enslavement to heroin. And we have felt more guilt for feeling relieved. We have beaten ourselves up for not being better parents even as we have resisted the assumptions that we are bad parents of "bad kids." All these experiences have overlain the profound grief that has shaped our lives and fashioned our futures.

As I described contemporary research about the grief process, I underscored the truth that grief has no timetable and no predictable stages, contrary to what was previously thought. Instead, there are tasks to accomplish in one's own time and on one's own terms. As grievers, we have to acknowledge the loss, react to the separation, recollect the deceased and the relationship, relinquish our old attachments, and move into our "new normal" without forgetting our old lives.[12] We must reinvest in new relationships and new activities and make it a priority to take care of ourselves in the midst of it all.

This self-care involves every aspect of our lives. We

learn how vulnerable we are both to physical and mental illness as a result of the extreme stress loss creates. Being intentional about our nutrition, exercise, sleep, relationships, emotions, and spirituality are critical ways of nurturing ourselves into hardiness and wholeness.

I explored the concept of resilience and how some people adapt to their child's death more easily than others do. Research suggests that family resilience after a crisis involves a combination of factors including other stressors and the pileup of demands the family faces when the crisis strikes, the resources (financial, educational, social) the family possesses, and the family's perceptions (views, assumptions, beliefs, narrative) about the crisis. These factors function together to predict adaptation to a major event such as the death of one's child. Individual factors also contribute to resiliency. We discovered that age, gender, developmental stage, culture, personal, relational, and spiritual strengths affect individual adaptation to loss. Moreover, most people can develop some degree of resilience by tapping into past successes and developing new practices such as mindfulness, meditation, and empathy. The good news is that most people adapt and reconcile themselves to the losses they experience and go on to live fruitful and meaningful lives.

Unfortunately, a small percentage of people have a more difficult time managing the loss. Sometimes there are preexisting emotional or psychological problems that complicate the grief experience. Those suffering from this prolonged grief have a difficult time accepting the death, yearn for the deceased, cannot bear to speak of the deceased, and may be preoccupied with the deceased or the means of death. These folks have a pervasive sense of emptiness and sorrow, feel bitter or angry, cannot find meaning in life, and sometimes wish to die themselves. For those experiencing this intense, unrelenting grief reaction, professional counseling is advisable.

Making meaning from our child's death is the most important task we can engage in that leads to our healing. In this process, we come to terms with all our questions about *why* our child died. Then we create a narrative of our child's life and death. In this process, we learn that although we cannot control the circumstances of our lives, we can control our attitudes toward those circumstances and the meaning we make of them. I described several ways of remembering by doing that involve activities we can engage in that help us accomplish this important task. Some of these activities include confronting stigma surrounding our child's death, becoming more assertive, engaging in rituals and symbols that honor our deceased children, creating memory collections, journaling, and blogging.

Confronting the issues and questions that arise from our religious or spiritual beliefs is also part of the making sense of our loss. Some of us discover that our previously held beliefs are inadequate for addressing such a significant, life-altering loss, and we turn away from them. Some of us find ourselves enraged at God, struggling to understand how a loving God could permit such tragic suffering.

Others find comfort and solace in a faith that supersedes logical explanations or theories. They find their beliefs are strong enough to withstand the terrible storm. Others of us cannot come to any reasonable spiritual or religious answer to our questions. Some are content to live in the mystery of not knowing. They focus not on *why* this tragic loss occurred but rather on how to respond now that it has happened.

On the other side of this tremendous grief, those making their way forward often are able to point to some positive outcomes or benefits that have emerged. In the crucible of crisis we learn so much about ourselves and other people. We learn how strong we really are. We realize our grief process involves both turning toward the loss and turning away from it. We discover on whom we can depend and who cannot tolerate our pain. We uncover qualities in our families and ourselves that contribute to our resilience. We learn what research reveals about the characteristics associated with improved life, health, well-being, and longevity, and we understand how cultivating them can ease our grief. We revisit gratitude on a grand scale, celebrating all we have been given rather than focusing on all we have lost. We become intimately aware of the multitude of gifts our deceased child gave us, and we commit ourselves to carrying on that legacy.

When I reflect on my grief journey, I think of my ankle fracture as a metaphor for the healing of my broken heart. When I broke my ankle in three places, it required surgery that involved plates, pins, and screws. Ironically, with all that titanium inside, it is stronger than before I fractured it. So it is with my personal fortitude. I have found myself to be stronger than I ever imagined precisely *because* of the brokenness. Although my ankle functions quite well most of the time and allows me to engage in rigorous hiking and challenging workouts, I have to anticipate times when it will be stressed. If I am planning a long hike over uneven, rocky terrain, I know I will need to ice and elevate my ankle later in the day. Likewise, on the difficult days such as Cameron's birthday, Mother's Day, the anniversary of his death, and holidays, I know I will feel particularly sad and vulnerable and I will need to anticipate these feelings. I have learned to be intentional about planning nurturing activities and surrounding myself with supportive, loving people. Having spent nearly four months immobilized with a fractured ankle, I now have heightened empathy for anyone using crutches, a knee scooter, or a wheelchair. I know how difficult it is to navigate curbs, uneven sidewalks, and wet pavement. I, too, have struggled with doors too heavy to be opened and have waited patiently for someone to notice I needed help. Similarly, I know the depth of pain associated with losing a child or another loved one because I have had the experience. As a result, I am quick to anticipate what another mourner may be experiencing and to offer assistance. Although my ankle fracture has healed completely, sometimes without warning, I feel a familiar stab of pain in that joint. It isn't debilitating; I don't usually lose my balance; and so far, I haven't fallen. So it is with my grief. There are always unexpected triggers that cause a familiar pain to shoot through my heart: a mother coming out of the grocery story with a child's birthday cake, a package of plaid boxer shorts in a department store, the aroma of eggs Benedict at the local diner, the strains of Leonard Cohen's "Hallelujah" –the music played when we scattered Cameron's ashes. All these moments send twinges of grief through me. They do not shatter me or interfere with my ability to function. They are simply reminders of both the pain and the love that will last a lifetime.

The Japanese art form *Kintsugi* is the process whereby fractured Japanese bowls are repaired. Most people would like such damages to be hidden, so when repaired they look like new. But Kintsugi follows a different philosophy. Rather than concealing the breakage, Kintsugi restores the broken item by incorporating the damage into the aesthetic of the restored item, making it part of the object's history. Kintsugi uses lacquer resin mixed with powdered gold, silver, platinum, copper or bronze, resulting in something more beautiful than the original.[13]

All of us who have experienced the death of a child are like the Japanese bowls. There are cracks and scars in our lives we have no need to hide. Through our grief journeys, those fractures have been filled with the gold of resilience, the gold of support and love, the gold of spirituality, the gold of making meaning of loss, the gold of gratitude, the gold of remembrance. During the difficult days when we are aware of the brokenness and the grief, may we, the ones left behind, also remember the gold that fills our emptiness and makes us shine.

QUESTIONS FOR REFLECTION:

» On the other side of loss, how have you changed individually? Relationally? Emotionally? Spiritually? What are the indicators of those changes? How have the changes made you more or less equipped to integrate your grief into your "new normal"?

» What are the ways you have continued to grow as you piece together your life?

» How important is gratitude in your life now? In what tangible ways do you practice it?

» Who needs your forgiveness? Where are you on the path of forgiveness? What are your next steps?

» How have you been courageous during your grief process? In what ways does your courage give you strength to move forward in your life?

» How important is humor for managing grief? Does it come easily to you? If not, how do you struggle with it?

» How do you extend kindness to others and to yourself? How could you engage in acts of kindness in memory of your child?

» How deeply have you developed compassion? In what ways have you been able to extend compassion to yourself?

» How have you invited expressiveness to show itself in your life? What are the ways you unleash your creativity? How have you used this creativity in adapting to your life after loss?

Appendix A: Resources for the Grief Journey

Books on Grief

Bowler, K. (2018). *Everything happens for a reason: And other lies I've loved.* **New York: Random House.**
Written by a Duke University divinity school professor diagnosed with stage IV colon cancer, this author describes all of the unhelpful things people unwittingly say to people who are dying. Bowler characterizes the types of people who make these painful comments as minimizers, teachers, and solvers. She offers a personal narrative of her struggle and responses to these difficult comments.

Levine, S. (2005). *Unattended sorrow: Recovering from loss and reviving the heart.* **Emmaus, PA: Rodale Books.**
Unattended sorrow is unresolved grief that has been squelched and repressed so it cannot be addressed. This spiritually oriented book assists those who are reeling from a significant loss to come to terms with it so they do not become stuck and unable to find joy in their lives.

Neimeyer, R. A. (2006). *Lessons of loss: A guide to coping.* **Memphis, TN: Robert A. Neimeyer.**
In *Lessons of Loss*, the author explores grief reactions and discusses the challenges grievers face as they navigate various types of loss. The book focuses on grievers, helpers, and offers personal applications.

Richardson, J. (2016). *The Cure for Sorrow: A Book of Blessings for Times of Grief.* **Orlando, FL: Wanton Gospeller Press.**
When Jan Richardson's husband and creative partner died suddenly she responded by doing what she had been doing already: writing blessings. From the vortex of her grief she offered her pain and also grace and hope. These blessings underscore the power of love that is "sorrow's most lasting cure."

Wolfelt, A. D. (2003). *Understanding your grief: Ten essential touchstones for finding hope and healing in your heart.* **Ft. Collins, CO: Companion Press.**
Wolfelt describes the unique factors in each person's grief and normalizes thoughts and feelings associated with grief. Wolfelt addresses spirituality and religion and provides opportunities for grievers to write about their grief experiences.

Wolterstorff, N. (1987). *Lament for a son.* **Grand Rapids, MI: William B. Eerdmans.**
The author describes the progress of his grief, from the

shock of learning of his son's accidental death to his integration of it a year later.

Books on Mindfulness and Meditation

Kabat-Zinn, J. (1994). *Wherever you go, there you are: Mindfulness meditation in everyday life.* **NY: Hyperion.**
Jon Kabat-Zinn, renowned scientist and meditation guru, teaches readers how to practice mindfulness in everyday life.

Kornfield, J. (1993). *A path with heart.* **New York: Bantam Books.**
Buddhist teacher and meditation master Jack Kornfield teaches readers how to deepen their spirituality through mindfulness and meditation. The specific meditations are useful for both beginners and those seasoned in the practice of meditation.

Organizations

Bereaved Parents of USA (https://bereavedparentsusa.org)
Bereaved Parents of the USA (BPUSA) is a national nonprofit self-help group that offers support, understanding, compassion and hope to bereaved

parents, grandparents or siblings struggling to rebuild their lives after the death of their children, grandchildren or siblings. There are no dues or fees to become a member of BPUSA and there are no paid salaries within the organization. All work is done by volunteer bereaved parents. These volunteers have a strong desire to help other families survive the death of their children just as they were helped when their own children died (from the Bereaved Parents USA website).

Compassionate Friends
http://compassionatefriends.org

The Compassionate Friends provides highly personal comfort, hope, and support to every family experiencing the death of a son or a daughter, a brother or a sister, or a grandchild, and helps others better assist the grieving family.

The Compassionate Friends was founded over 40 years ago when a chaplain at the Warwickshire Hospital in England brought together two sets of grieving parents and realized that the support they gave each other was better than anything he, as a chaplain, could ever say or provide. Meeting around a kitchen table, the Lawleys and the Hendersons were joined by a bereaved mother and the chaplain, Simon Stephens, and The Society of the Compassionate Friends was born. The Compassionate Friends jumped across the ocean and was established in the United States and incorporated in 1978 in Illinois. Each chapter, along with the supporting National Office, is committed to helping every bereaved parent, sibling, or grandparent who may walk through our doors or contact us. (from the Compassionate Friends website)

Mothers in Sympathy and Support
www.missfoundations.org

The MISS Foundation, established in 1996 by Dr. Joanne Cacciatore, is an international 501(c)3, volunteer-based organization providing C.A.R.E. [counseling, advocacy, research, and education] services to families experiencing the death of a child. We promote a non-medicalized, community-based approach to grief including equine therapy with rescue horses, eco therapies through retreats and activities in nature, and mindfulness practices such as meditation and yoga. (from the MISS website)

NOPE: Narcotics Overdose Prevention and Education
www.nopetaskforce.org

The mission of NOPE is to diminish the frequency and impact of overdose death through community education, family support and purposeful advocacy.

WEBSITES

www.aftertalk.com

An online resource containing blogs, inspirational quotes, interactive writing tools, and an opportunity to ask questions of an internationally known grief expert.

www.grasphelp.org
(Grief Recovery After Substance Passing)

An online support group for those who have lost someone to a substance overdose.

www.onlinegriefsupport.com/group/losing-someone-to-drug-overdose

An online support group for those who have lost someone to a substance overdose.

www.cathytaughinbaugh.com/when-addiction-wins-support-for-grieving-families

An online support group for parents who have lost a child to a drug overdose.

www.healingheart.net/penpals/child-adult/child_overdose4.html

A website listing contact information for parents who have lost a child to a drug overdose. Others may request pen pals from the group to share stories and offer support.

www.griefnet.org

A general grief-related website with email support groups and resources.

www.sandyswenson.com

A website for support for mothers who have lost their children to addiction.

MINDFULNESS AND MEDITATION WEBSITES

www.headspace.com
This website has an app for smartphone or tablets. The first sessions are free on a trial basis. Ongoing use requires a subscription.

www.calm.com
This website is intended to reduce anxiety, improve sleep, and help people feel happier. It offers free sessions and a subscription for ongoing use.

About the Author

Dr. Marsha Wiggins is a professional counselor, author, educator, consultant, public speaker, and retired clergywoman. She has published over 50 articles in professional journals and is the author of *Integrating Religion and Spirituality into Counseling: A Comprehensive Approach* (Brooks/Cole, 2003). She is the recipient of a writing award from the Association of Spiritual, Ethical and Religious Values in Counseling.

Dr. Wiggins is the Executive Director of the Association for Counselor Education and Supervision (ACES) and Professor Emerita of Counseling at the University of Colorado Denver. She earned a Master of Divinity degree from Emory University and a Ph.D. from the University of Florida.

Dr. Wiggins is also a mother who lost her 26-year-old son to a heroin overdose. She knows both professionally and personally what it is like to experience this unique form of grief.

In her leisure time, she likes to travel, hike, cook, read, and play any kind of word game! Visit her at www.drmarshawiggins.com or follow her on Twitter @MarshaWiggins1.

NOTES

Chapter 2

1. Neugarten, B. L. (1969). Continuities and discontinuities of psychological issues into adult life. *Human Development, 12,* 121-130.
2. http://www.health.wa.gov.au/docreg/Education/ Population/Health_Problems/Mental_Illness/ Mentalhealth_stigma_fact.pdf. Retrieved July 19, 2017.
3. http://www.sandyswenson.com/addiction-quotes-parents-of-addicts/. Retrieved July 19, 2017.
4. Kreek, M. J., Nielsen, D. A., Butelman, E. R., & LaForge, K. S. (2005). Genetic influences on impulsivity, risk taking, stress sensitivity, and vulnerability to drug abuse and addiction. *Nature Neuroscience, 11,* (8), 1450-1457. doi: 10.1038/ nn1583.

Chapter 3

1. Elisabeth Kubler-Ross (1969). *On death and dying.* New York: The Macmillan Company.
2. Neimeyer, R. A. (Ed.)(2001). *Meaning making and the experience of loss.* Washington, DC: American Psychological Association.
3. Rando, T. (1983). An investigation of grief and adaptation in parents whose children have died from cancer. *Journal of Pediatric Psychology, 8,* 3-20.
4. Rando, T. (1983). An investigation of grief and adaptation in parents whose children have died from cancer. *Journal of Pediatric Psychology, 8,* 3-20.
5. Levine, S. (2005). *Unattended sorrow.* Emmaus, PA: Rodale, p. 101.
6. Wolterstorff, N. (1987). *Lament for a son.* Grand Rapids, MI: Erdmans, p. 26.
7. Strobe, M., & Schut, H A. W. (1999). The dual process model of coping with bereavement: Rationale and description. *Death Studies, 23,* 1-28.
8. Wijngaards-de Meij, L., Stroebe, M., Schut, H., Stroebe, W., van den Bout, J., van der Heijden, P., et al. (2007). Neuroticism and attachment insecurity as predictors of bereavement outcome. *Journal of Research in Personality, 41,* 498-505.

Chapter 4

1. See The Compassionate Friends website: www. compassionatefriends.org

2. Kornfield, J. (1993). *A path with heart: A guide through the perils and promises of spiritual life.* New York: Bantam.

Chapter 5

1. Hooeyman, N. R., & Kramer, B. J. (2006). *Living through loss: Interventions across the life span.* New York: Columbia University Press.
2. Sandberg, S. & Grant, A. (2017). *Option B: Facing adversity, building resilience, and finding joy.* New York: Alfred A. Knopf.
3. Patterson, Joan M. (2002). Understanding family resilience. *Journal of Clinical Psychology, 58*(3), 233-246. doi: 10.1002/jclp.10019
4. Patterson, J. M. (2002). Understanding family resilience. *Journal of Clinical Psychology, 58*(3), 233-246. doi: 10.1002/jclp.10019
5. Patterson, Joan M. (2002). Understanding family resilience. *Journal of Clinical Psychology, 58*(3), 233-246. doi: 10.1002/jclp.10019
6. Greeff, A. P., Vansteenwegen, A., & Herbiest, T. (2011). Indicators of family resilience after the death of a child. *OMEGA, 63*(4), 343-356.
7. Graham, L. (2013). *Bouncing Back: Rewiring your brain for maximum resilience and well-being.* Novato, CA: New World Library.
8. Zolli, A. (2012, November 2). Learning to bounce back. *New York Times,* Opinion.
9. Megginson, L. (1963, June). Lessons from Europe for American Business. *Southwestern Social Science Quarterly, 44*(1), (Presidential address delivered at the Southwestern Social Science Association convention in

San Antonio, Texas, April 12, 1963), p. 4.

10. Fabrega, M. 14 Ways to be more resilient so you can bounce back from adversity. Daringtolivefully.com/be-more-resilient. Retrieved February 21, 2018

11. Southwick, S., & Chaney, D. (2012). *Resilience: The science of mastering life's greatest challenges.* Cambridge, United Kingdom: Cambridge University Press.

12. Graham, L. (2013). *Bouncing Back: Rewiring your brain for maximum resilience and well-being.* Novato, CA: New World Library.

13. Koren, L. (2008). *Wabi-Sabi: For artists, designers, poets, and philosophers.* Point Reyes, CA: Imperfect Publishing.

Chapter 6

1. Kersting, A., Brahler, E., Glaesmer, H., & Wagner, B. (2011). Prevalence of complicated grief in a representative population-based sample. *Journal of Affective Disorders, 131,* 339-343.
2. American Psychiatric Association (2013). *Diagnostic and statistical manual of mental disorders: DSM-5* (5th ed.). Arlington, VA: Author.
3. Fleming, S. (2012). Complicated grief and trauma: What to treat first? (pp. 83-85). In R. A. Neimeyer, (Ed.), *Techniques of Grief Therapy: Creative Practices for Counseling the Bereaved.* New York: Routledge.
4. Wolfelt, A. D. (2003). *Understanding your grief: Ten essential touchstones for finding hope and healing in your heart.* Ft. Collins, CO: Companion.
5. Kersting, A., Kroker, K., Horstmann, J., Ohrmann, P., Baune, B. T., Arolt, V., & Suslow, T. (2009). Complicated grief in patients with unipolar depression. *Journal of Affective Disorders, 118,* 201-204.
6. Kersting, A., Kroker, K., Horstmann, J., Ohrmann, P., Baune, B. T., Arolt, V., & Suslow, T. (2009). Complicated grief in patients with unipolar depression. *Journal of Affective Disorders, 118,* 201-204.
7. American Psychiatric Association (2013). *Diagnostic and statistical manual of mental disorders: DSM-5* (5th ed.). Arlington, VA: Author.

8. Rando, T. A. (2011). "Is it okay for you to be okay?" (pp. 149-151). In R. A. Neimeyer, (Ed.), *Techniques of Grief Therapy: Creative Practices for Counseling the Bereaved.* New York: Routledge.

Chapter 7

1. Lichtenthal, W. G., Currier, J. M., Neimeyer, R. A., Keesee, N. J. (2010). Sense and significance: A mixed methods examination of meaning making after the loss of one's child. *Journal of Clinical Psychology, 66*(7), 791-812. doi: 10.1002/jclp.20700.
2. Neimeyer, R. A., (2001). *Meaning reconstruction and the experience of loss.* Washington, DC: American Psychological Association.
3. Neimeyer, R. A. (2002). *Lessons of loss: A guide to coping* (2nd ed). New York: Routledge. Murphy, S. A., Johnson, L. C., Lohan, J. (2003). Finding meaning in a child's violent death: A five-year prospective analysis of parents' personal narratives and empirical data. *Death Studies, 27*(5), 381–404.
4. Kreek, M. J., Mielsen, D. A., Butelman, E. R., La Forge, K. S. (2005). Genetic influences on impulsivity, risk-taking, stress-responsivity and vulnerability to drug abuse and addiction. *Nature Neuroscience, 8*(11), 1450-1458.
5. Kreek, M. J., Mielsen, D. A., Butelman, E. R., La Forge, K. S. (2005). Genetic influences on impulsivity, risk-taking, stress-responsivity and vulnerability to drug abuse and addiction. *Nature Neuroscience, 8*(11), 1450-1458.
6. Squeglia, L. M., Jacobus, J., & Taupert, S. F.

(2009). The influence of substance abuse on adolescent brain development. *Clinical EEG neuroscience, 40*(1), 31-38.

7. Squeglia, L. M., Jacobus, J., & Taupert, S. F. (2009). The influence of substance abuse on adolescent brain development. *Clinical EEG neuroscience, 40*(1), 31-38.

8. Squeglia, L. M., Jacobus, J., & Taupert, S. F. (2009). The influence of substance abuse on adolescent brain development. *Clinical EEG neuroscience, 40*(1), 31-38.

9. Kreek, M. J., Levran, O., Reed, B., Schlussman, S. D., Zhoi, Y., & Butelman, E. R. (2012). Opiate addiction and cocaine addiction: Underlying molecular neurobiology and genetics. *Journal of Clinical Investigation,* (10), 3387-3393.

10. Johnson, S. W., & North, R. A. (1992). Opioids excite dopamine neurons by hyperpolarization of local interneurons. *Journal of Neuroscience,* 12(2), 483-488.

11. Quinones, S. (2015). *Dreamland: The True Tale of America's Opiate Epidemic.* New York: Bloomsbury.

12. www.vox.com/policy-and-politics/2017/6/6/15743986/opioid-epidemic-overdose-deaths-2016. Retrieved December 5, 2017.

13. Mitchell, P. "Theodicy overview. https://www3.dbu.edu/mitchell/theodicy.htm. Retrieved December 5, 2017.

14. Weatherhead, L. D. (1944/1972). *The Will of God.* Nashville, TN: Abingdon.

15. https://en.wikipedia.org/wiki/Eschatology. Retrieved December 6, 2017.

16. Kushner, H. S. (1981). *When Bad Things Happen to Good People.* New York: Anchor. p. 54.

17. Weatherhead, L. D. (1972). *The Will of God.* Nashville, TN: Abingdon. p. 22.

18. Frankl, V. E. (1959/1992). *Man's search for meaning* (revised ed.). Boston: Beacon, p. 75.

19. Irion, M. J. (1970). *Yes, world: A mosaic of meditation.* New York: Richard W. Baron Publishing Company, Inc. p. 88.

20. Lichtenthal, W. G., & Neimeyer, R. A. (2012). Directed journaling to facilitate meaning making. In R. A. Neimeyer, (ed.). *Techniques of grief therapy: Creative practices for counseling the bereaved.* NY: Routledge.

Chapter 8

1. Quinones, S. *Dreamland: The True Tale of America's Opiate Epidemic.* NY: Bloomsbury.

2. Potash, J. S., & Handel, S. (2012). Memory boxes (pp. 243-246). In R. A. Neimeyer, (ed.), *Techniques of grief therapy: Creative practices for counseling the bereaved.* New York: Routledge.

3. Berger, J. (2012). Playing with playlists (pp. 211-214). In R. A. Neimeyer, (ed.), *Techniques of grief therapy: Creative practices for counseling the bereaved.* New York: Routledge.

4. Loomis, M. http://www.buildyourownblog.net/. Retrieved December 19, 2017.

Chapter 9

1. Calhoun, L. G. & Tedeschi, R. G. (2001). Post-traumatic growth: The positive lessons of loss (pp. 157-172). In Neimeyer, R. A. (ed). *Meaning reconstruction and the experience of loss.* Washington, DC: American Psychological Association.
2. Frantz, T. T., Trolley B. C., & Johll, M. P. (1996). Religious aspects of bereavement. *Pastoral Psychology, 44*(3), 151-163.
3. Frantz, T. T., Farrell, M. M., & Trolley, B. (2001). Positive outcomes of losing a loved one (pp. 191-209). In Neimeyer, R. A. (ed). *Meaning reconstruction and the experience of loss.* Washington, DC: American Psychological Association.
4. Post, S. & Neimark, J. (2007). *Why good things happen to good people.* New York: Broadway Books.
5. Post, S. & Neimark, J. (2007). *Why good things happen to good people.* New York: Broadway Books.
6. Dalai Lama Trust, Tutu, D., & Abrams, D. (2016). *The Book of Joy: Lasting Happiness in a Changing world.* New York: Penguin Random House.
7. Vilaythong, A. P., Arnau, R. C., Rosen, D. H., & Mascaro, N. (2003). Hope and humor: Can humor increase hope? *Humor, 16*(1), 79-89.
8. Herth, K. (1993). Hope in older adults in community and institutional settings. *Issues in Mental Health Nursing, 14*, 139-156.

9. Cacciatore, J. (2012). The kindness project (pp. 329-331). In R. A. Neimeyer (Ed.). *Techniques of grief therapy: Cognitive practices for counseling the bereaved.* NY: Routledge.

10. Jinpa, T. (2015). *A fearless heart: How the courage to be compassionate can Transform Our Lives.* New York: Penguin Random House.

11. The Rosemary Company. www.rosemarycompany. com.

12. Rando, T. (1983). An investigation of grief and adaptation in parents whose children have died from cancer. *Journal of Pediatric Psychology, 8,* 3-20.

13. Kaushik. "Kintsugi: The Japanese art of fixing broken pottery with gold. http://www. amusingplanet.com/2014/05/kintsugi-japanese-art-of-fixing-broken.html. Retrieved January 5, 2018.